A PENGUIN SPECIAL

Apartheid's Second Front

Dr Joseph Hanlon was correspondent in Mozambique for the BBC, the *Guardian* and for various financial magazines from 1979 to 1985. He is an expert in southern African politics and economics and has written: *Mozambique: The Revolution under Fire* (1984) and *SADCC: Progress, Projects and Prospects* (1985).

Commenting on Hanlon's Mozambique book, Tanzania's President Julius Nyerere wrote: 'None of us can ask for more than this kind of approach by those who write about our countries . . . I wish to congratulate you.'

D1509690

Apartheid's Second Front
South Africa's War against Its Neighbours

JOSEPH HANLON

PENGUIN BOOKS

Penguin Books Ltd, Harmondsworth, Middlesex, England
Viking Penguin Inc., 40 West 23rd Street, New York, New York 10010, U.S.A.
Penguin Books Australia Ltd, Ringwood, Victoria, Australia
Penguin Books Canada Limited, 2801 John Street, Markham, Ontario, Canada L3R 1B4
Penguin Books (N.Z.) Ltd, 182–190 Wairau Road, Auckland 10, New Zealand

First published 1986

Apartheid's Second Front is based on a more detailed
study, *Beggar Your Neighbours*, published by the Catholic
Institute for International Relations and James Currey,
copyright © Catholic Institute for International Relations,
1986.

Made and printed in Great Britain by
Richard Clay (The Chaucer Press) Ltd, Bungay, Suffolk
Typeset in Monophoto Plantin

Contents

List of maps

Introduction

In townships throughout South Africa there is a war being waged against apartheid. But South Africa's white leadership has concluded that the best way to preserve minority rule is to fight that war outside South Africa – to open up a 'second front' in the neighbouring states. The goal is nothing less than control of the neighbours. Pretoria intends to keep them in thrall and thus to create a buffer against both the southward tide of majority rule and against international campaigns for sanctions.

This is a curiously hidden war. In part, this is because South Africa's war against its neighbours combines military, economic, and political action in a mix that is usually called 'destabilization'. Activity in the neighbouring states is diffuse and often hidden, while actions inside South Africa grab the headlines. Yet in the past five years this has become a full-scale war, and casualties outside South Africa on the second front are vastly higher than those inside. Since 1980, the war on the second front has cost more than 100,000 lives and £10,000 million, and has made at least one million people homeless.

There are a number of unusual aspects of this war. The first is that it is extremely one-sided, which is perhaps why outsiders find it hard to believe just how hard South Africa is hitting its neighbours. South Africa's military might is substantially greater than that of all the neighbouring states combined. Yet, despite years of aggression, the military or security forces of the neighbouring states have never crossed into South Africa.

The second is that it is a largely economic war, with most

military actions aimed at effecting economic results. The neighbours have been made dependent on South Africa and the war is intended to keep them that way. This lends bizarre and confusing aspects to this war. Aggressor and victims are linked by direct-dial telephones, railways, and extensive trade. In February 1984, when leaders of the neighbouring states met in Lusaka, Zambia, to discuss reducing those links, they were transported to the conference hall in Mercedes Benz cars hastily imported from South Africa; delegates visited shops on Lusaka's Cairo Road to buy South African wine. Mozambique's capital, Maputo, was bombed by the South African Air Force, but the electricity, onions, and a variety of other goods still flow from South Africa to Maputo. Every state in the region exhibits similar ironies and contradictions, and a major purpose of this book is to explain the complex and confusing relationship between South Africa and its neighbours.

In its attempts to make the neighbouring states captive, South Africa uses a mixture of carrot and stick (or perhaps sjambok, the South African rhinoceros-hide whip used by the police in the townships). The carrot takes the form of economic incentives, trade links, jobs for miners, and outright bribery and corruption. The sjambok is the destabilization, which is intended to keep the neighbours in line, accepting the few carrots on offer.

The South African government will continue to sjambok its neighbours as long as it sjamboks its own people. The war against the neighbours will end only with the end of apartheid; only majority rule in South Africa can halt the destabilization. But since the war is being fought outside South Africa, as much as inside, the defeat of apartheid requires the support of those neighbouring states who are now the second front.

In the first chapter, I look at one day in the war: 9 December 1982. Next, in chapters 2–6, I try to explain South African government policy, and why white South Africa is waging a war against its neighbours. The war itself is discussed in chapters 7–13, followed by South Africa's fraudulent Nkomati non-aggression pact with Mozambique in chapter 14. Finally, in chapters 15 and 16, I ask what can be done to support the neighbours and to help bring majority rule to the region as a whole. In these last chapters, I look particularly at the issue of sanctions against South Africa. The British Foreign Office and 'liberal' white politicians inside South Africa often argue that sanctions against South Africa should not be used because they will only hurt the neighbours. I try to show that not only is this not true, but that the neighbouring states themselves are calling for sanctions.

Although South Africa has been attacking its neighbours, particularly Angola, for many years, the war only became widespread in late 1980, after the independence of Zimbabwe. I was a correspondent in Mozambique for the BBC, *Guardian*, and *Africa Economic Digest* from 1979 to 1985, and I remember well the optimism that greeted Zimbabwe's independence. For Mozambique and the other states in the region, the trauma of sanctions and war were over. It was time to build, to develop the region to benefit the people who lived there instead of the colonial powers. I saw people's initial disbelief turn slowly to the shocked realization that white South Africa could not and would not allow successful multiracial states on its doorstep. And I watched the dreams turn to dust – crushed by South Africa.

During my five years in Maputo, I also travelled throughout the region and wrote about the Southern African Development Coordination Conference (SADCC – pronounced Sad–ec), the economic organization of the majority-ruled states. This book is based on a year of research and extensive travel in 1985 in most of the countries of the region. (The research was funded by the Catholic Institute for International Relations (CIIR) in London.) This short account can only scrape the surface, point to many of the complex links between South Africa and its neighbours, show that apartheid has a second front, and demonstrate that there is a war going on in southern Africa. A much more detailed study of that investigation is to be published in 1986 as *Beggar Your Neighbours* (CIIR and James Currey). It will contain the full references and footnotes, which have been omitted here.

Special thanks must go to three people who contributed to the longer book, and whose material I have plundered for this one: Teresa Smart, Colin Stoneman, and John Daniel. Thanks also to Paul Spray of CIIR and to the dozens of people in southern Africa who provided essential information and advice.

March 1986

Chapter One

9 December 1982

Simultaneously, the commandos stormed a dozen flats and houses, hitting the enemy with machine-gun fire, rockets, and grenades. Some were slaughtered in their beds, perhaps before they knew what was happening. Others were shot as they tried to flee. Safeta Jafeta begged for mercy for his wife and family, but all were slain, including their two-year-old child.

The raid shattered the moonlit stillness of Lesotho's capital Maseru, on the early morning of 9 December 1982. By sunrise, forty-two people had been killed – thirty South African refugees and twelve Basotho (Lesotho nationals), like Safeta Jafeta and his family. Later General Constand Viljoen, head of the South African Defence Force (SADF), said that the seven women and three children had been 'killed in the cross-fire'.

More than a hundred South African commandos took part. Some arrived in helicopters with their equipment. But others brazenly stayed the night at the Victoria Hotel on the main street, then simply climbed the hill behind the hotel to attack the modern Koena Flats. In number 28 they splintered the door with machine-gun fire and sprayed the inside with bullets, killing a 21-year-old Basotho woman, Matume Ralebitso. The daughter of a former cabinet minister and ambassador to Mozambique, she had only moved into her town-centre flat a month before, following her graduation from Lesotho University where she had been the best student of the year.

Most of the dead were South African refugees. Some were simply students and others with no political links. But some of the dead were members of the African National Congress, including the country representative, Zola Nqini, who had gone to Lesotho in 1978 after serving a twelve-year sentence on Robben Island. In defending the raid at the United Nations a week later, South African Ambassador David Steward said the raid had been against ANC 'bases for launching acts of violence against South Africa'.

Foreign press touring the smashed and burned homes found no evidence of bases. Prime Minister Leabua Jonathan asked why, if these really were bases, South Africa had not asked Lesotho to deal with them during regular meetings between Lesotho and South African ministers and officials; after all, they had brought up much more trivial issues like ANC leaflets being printed in Lesotho. Nineteen Canadian doctors working in Lesotho wrote in an open letter that the 'homes were highly visible, situated on public thoroughfares, and any military activity would have been immediately apparent'. And they pointed out that 'men, women and children alike were slaughtered. Among the critically injured was one woman six months pregnant who was shot in the abdomen.'

The raid did not go quite to plan, however. In the middle of an 8 a.m. briefing for foreign diplomats, Foreign Minister Charles D. Molapo was summoned to the phone to be told by the head of the Lesotho army that sixty-four commandos were still in Lesotho, and were only then being picked up by South African helicopters. Prime Minister Jonathan later told parliament that 'the South Africans phoned our forces to say that some of their men were missing, and that if we were holding them we should release them without delay, failing which . . . we would have been bombarded by the South African Air Force'. Far from being captured, the commandos had simply lost their way and missed their lift home.

After the raid, the recriminations. It soon became clear that South Africa had allies inside Lesotho. The twelve houses in the raid had been carefully selected. For example, Matume Ralebitso was living in the flat that had been occupied by the former ANC representative, Martin Hani, until he left Lesotho two months before. Someone had shown the South Africans the way, and it was noted that several months before the raid Lesotho security officers had searched many ANC houses and confiscated a variety of ANC literature.

It was also obvious that the Lesotho security forces did nothing to intervene or stop the raid. Indeed, there were press reports that they had cleared the streets of late-night travellers before the raid. One of the South African organizers of the raid, General Gleeson, claimed that he 'managed to reach the commander of the Lesotho forces to [successfully] request them to withdraw, after informing them that our operation was solely aimed at the ANC'. Lesotho officials initially denied this, but later admitted that *some* people had had advance warning.

In a statement to parliament, Prime Minister Jonathan declared 'that South Africa has infiltrated even our government ministries'. In private, high officials go further, and allege that some members of the government had prior knowledge of the raid. Several months later, Charles D. Molapo resigned as foreign minister, and on 5 January 1984 he was part of a group of Basotho politicians who set up an opposition party – at a meeting with the South African foreign minister, Pik Botha, in Pretoria.

As well as officials and the security services knowing in advance about the raid, Lesotho officials allege that the United States knew too, and withdrew its people from Maseru the night of the raid.

And in Mozambique

At exactly the same time that one group of South African commandos was attacking Maseru, another group was at work 800 miles away in Beira, Mozambique. They destroyed a fuel depot in the port, causing more than £15 million damage. The fuel was intended to be sent to Zimbabwe and Malawi. The Beira–Zimbabwe oil pipeline had reopened just six months before. Until then, Zimbabwe had been largely dependent on South Africa for fuel – an inheritance of the years of sanctions against UDI Rhodesia. South Africa had used the control to put political pressure on Zimbabwe, for example in September 1981 when the South Africans delayed fuel trains for Zimbabwe, causing a petrol shortage.

The pipeline threatened South Africa's stranglehold over Zimbabwe's fuel. So South African-backed anti-Frelimo MNR rebels attacked the pipeline. Zimbabwe responded in late 1982 by sending its own troops into Mozambique to guard the pipe. South Africa answered with the 9 December direct attack on the tank farm.

Zimbabwe had alternative routes – fuel could be railed from the refinery in Maputo either directly or via the line through north-eastern South Africa. The former route had been used until the pipeline was reopened, and was pressed into use again. But that line runs parallel to the South African border through more than 200 miles of semi-desert. It is an easy target: South African-controlled MNR rebels came over the border and attacked the line at about the same time as the tanks were hit. Some fuel got through, but Mozambique railways lost a number of tank wagons.

This left the old UDI sanctions-busting route via South Africa, which already carried aviation fuel and specialist oil products from Maputo to Zimbabwe. These could not be sent through the pipeline and Zimbabwe's jumbo tank wagons were too large for the direct route, so the longer South Africa route was still in use for three trains of fuel a week.

As an emergency measure, Zimbabwe put ordinary petrol and diesel in some of the jumbo tankers. But South Africa cut off that line as well. Trains left Maputo and entered South Africa, but never emerged again. Virtually no fuel reached Zimbabwe, and there were queues of cars at the petrol stations. South Africa said that it was happy to solve the fuel crisis – if Zimbabwe would do two things it had refused to do, namely send a minister to South Africa for discussions (Zimbabwe had always refused to have high-level political meetings with the apartheid state), and sign a new long-term fuel-supply agreement (ensuring permanent dependence on South Africa for fuel, when the whole exercise had been to break that dependence).

South Africa reinforced its attack in the most petty ways. For example, motorists driving from South Africa to Zimbabwe were stopped at roadblocks just before the border and told they were not allowed to carry cans of petrol or oil over the border.

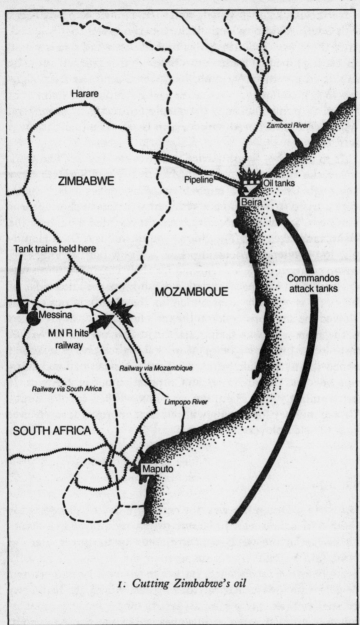

1. Cutting Zimbabwe's oil

Nevertheless, Zimbabwe held out, threatening a complete break with South African railways if the fuel trains were not released. After three weeks, South Africa backed down and said it would release the nine fuel trains it was holding; three turned out to be stabled in a yard in Messina, just over the border from Zimbabwe. The following week technicians completed a temporary system to pump fuel into the pipeline directly from tankers, bypassing the shattered tank farm in Beira. The fuel crisis was over.

As in Lesotho, South Africa had its allies inside. The week before the raid, employees of Manica Freight Services (now Renfreight), the largest freight forwarding agency in Beira port, were warned to fill their cars with petrol because a shortage was imminent. It was an arrogant move that revealed the role of the Manica management. The Beira head of Manica, Dion Hamilton, and his deputy, Benjamin Fox, are now both serving long prison sentences in Mozambique for their roles. Hamilton was a private pilot and parachutist who had immense knowledge of the port; it was his information to the South Africans that allowed the sea-borne raid on the tank farm. Fox was identified as the man who was taking arms and instructions to MNR bases in the bush near Beira. Manica Freight Services was then owned jointly by Safmarine, the South African national shipping line, and Anglo-American Corporation of South Africa. It seems unlikely that Hamilton and Fox worked for the South African military for so long without tacit approval at some level from their employers.

Not all successes

Thursday 9 December was not entirely a day of successes for South Africa, however. In Harare two men captured in a shoot-out earlier in the week were presented to the press. Benson Dube said he had been a member of the Rhodesian security forces before independence. Earlier in the year he had crossed illegally into South Africa, looking for work. He had been arrested and taken to a camp, where he underwent six months' training with fifty other Zimbabweans. He was part of a group of fifteen sent into Zimbabwe for a series of raids. Once north of the border, the group passed through the village of Zweli-banze Nzuma, a former guerrilla with Joshua Nkomo's Zapu. Nzuma was the second man at the press conference, and he said that he had recognized one of the men in the group as a former Zapu guerrilla, and that they had weapons like the ones he had in training in Angola. They had asked Nzuma to join them, and he did. 'I was willing to go back to the bush and fight,' Nzuma said. 'I was going to fight for Nkomo, because I wanted to see him back in parliament.' The following year, Dube and Nzuma were sentenced to death by the High Court for killing a police-man in the shoot-out in which they were captured.

South Africa was caught out again two days later on Saturday 11 December when a South African plane carrying businessmen from the Unita-held part of south-east Angola was shot down over Botswana. The plane had illegally crossed the border near the Caprivi strip of Namibia, which separates north-western Botswana from Angola. One of the men on the plane represented Frama Inter-trading, a Johannesburg firm with close links to the South African military. Frama flies supplies to Unita in Angola and the MNR in Mozambique, while it smuggles mil-lions of pounds of timber, diamonds, other precious stones, and ivory out of Angola and Mozambique. So the downing of a plane again exposed South Africa's secret support for the MNR and Unita.

In Angola itself, the war continued unabated. But on Monday 13 December, in one of the biggest raids in several months, four South African Air Force Mirages bombed the tiny railway town of Bilala, in southern Angola.

There is a war going on

In these few days of December 1982, Lesotho, Zimbabwe, Mozambique, Malawi, and Angola were all targets of South African destabilization. These actions combined political, econ-omic, and military pressure by using corporations, South African railways, agents in the governments of neighbouring states, its surrogate military forces in Mozambique and Angola, and its own commandos. It was a dramatic display of the war South Africa is waging against its neighbours.

South Africa has a long history of intervention in neighbouring states. It provided clandestine military and diplomatic support to the Katanga and Biafra secessionist movements in 1961 and 1967–70, respectively. In 1974 South Africa tried to capitalize on dissent in south-western Zambia, the former Barotseland, when it provided training in Namibia for Adamson Mushala and some of his followers, and sent them back into Zambia the following year. For seven years, the Mushala Gang was active in western Zambia, until Mushala was finally killed on 26 November 1982 – just two weeks before the dramatic events recounted in this chapter.

But isolated intervention has now been replaced by full-scale war. Faced with an uprising inside and majority rule outside the country, South Africa's white leadership has concluded that it can defend apartheid only by creating a second front and fighting a war beyond its borders.

Chapter Two

The tide of majority rule

The southbound tide of decolonization and majority rule has always been an intrinsic threat to white rule in South Africa. But for many years white South Africa was sheltered. Independence came to this region slowly and even today two of the eleven countries of southern Africa – Namibia and South Africa itself – have minority rule.

When Tanzania became the first independent majority-ruled state in 1961, it was really too far away to be a threat to Pretoria. Majority rule moved closer when Malawi and Zambia became independent in 1964.

The three smallest states in the region, Botswana, Lesotho, and Swaziland, came to independence in 1966 and 1968; generally known as the 'BLS states', these former British protectorates were especially closely tied to South Africa by the colonial rulers. Together they have just over three million people. Lesotho is a geographic anomaly: it is totally surrounded by South Africa and it is the only country in the world entirely above 1,400 metres (4,600 feet) in altitude.

That left white rule in four colonies, plus South Africa itself. And in sharp contrast to the relatively peaceful transition to majority rule in the other six states, whites in the remaining five countries resolved to fight to retain control. Twenty years later, that struggle is still going on.

The four white-governed colonies were Angola and Mozambique, still ruled by Portugal; Namibia, controlled by South Africa; and Zimbabwe, where white settlers under Ian Smith in 1965 announced a Unilateral Declaration of Independence (UDI) rather than permit Britain to institute majority rule in the then Rhodesia. The United Nations called for inter-

2. *Southern Africa*

Table 1: Basic data on southern Africa

COUNTRY	POPULATION (MILLION) (1985 EST.)	AREA (1,000 SQ KM)	DATE OF INDEPENDENCE
Angola	8.4	1,246	1975
Botswana	1.1	852	1966
Lesotho	1.5	30	1966
Malawi	7.0	95	1964
Mozambique	14.0	786	1975
Swaziland	0.6	17	1968
Tanzania	20.8	945	1961
Zambia	6.6	753	1964
Zimbabwe	8.2	391	1980
Total for nine majority-ruled states	68.2	5,115	
Namibia	1.5	823	still occupied by South Africa
South Africa	32.0	1,221	

and the population of South Africa is divided by the Pretoria government into these groups:

'African'	23.4	(of whom five million are assigned to the four 'independent' bantustans)
'White'	4.8	
'Coloured'	2.9	
'Indian'	0.9	

national sanctions against the Rhodesian settler regime. These were publicly supported by Britain, but privately the British government allowed the breaking of the key oil embargo, which permitted the Smith regime to survive for fifteen years. South Africa gave Rhodesia and Portugal economic and military help to defend white rule, and to create what it called a 'cordon sanitaire' of white-ruled states holding back the tide of majority rule.

Three of the independent states – Tanzania, Zambia, and Botswana – formed the frontline states to support their brothers and sisters still struggling for majority rule. (The other three states – Malawi, Swaziland, and Lesotho – were generally seen as more sympathetic to South Africa and to the Portuguese in Mozambique.)

Portugal's African wars cost it £3,000 million and 5,000 dead in fifteen years. The Portuguese army, weary of a fight that could not be won, overthrew the Lisbon government on 25 April 1974. Mozambique and Angola came to independence under Marxist governments the following year, but in very different ways. In Mozambique, Frelimo was the only independence movement and it took power unopposed.

Angola – paranoia justified

Angola was different. It is potentially one of the richest countries in Africa, with diamonds and massive offshore oil reserves, and there was United States and South African opposition to black Marxist rule there. Anyone who thinks African statesmen are unfairly paranoid about the CIA should read *In Search of Enemies* (W. W. Norton, New York, 1978) by John Stockwell, the former chief of the CIA Angola task force, who tells in horrifying detail what he did there a decade ago.

In Angola there were three liberation movements: the MPLA, which was Marxist and the most militarily effective; Unita, under Jonas Savimbi; and the FNLA, based in Zaire. The CIA had helped to put Mobutu in power in Zaire in 1965 and it also backed the FNLA. By 1969 Unita had established links with the Portuguese PIDE secret police; in 1971 Unita and the Portuguese military came to a secret agreement under which Unita would fight the MPLA instead of the Portuguese, in exchange for a role in the neo-colonial government it was hoped would result. At first the CIA refused to support Unita, because of its Chinese links. With the 1974 coup in Portugal, both the CIA and South Africa threw their weight behind the FNLA and Unita to prevent the MPLA taking power. By 9 November a joint FNLA–Zaire army and CIA–South African column reached within twelve miles of the capital, Luanda, in an effort to capture it on independence day, 11 November. South Africa flew in long-range artillery and gunners, who began shelling the capital.

Stockwell tells how CIA and South African observers sat on a ridge to watch the capture of Luanda, while in CIA headquarters near Washington, the Angola task force decorated its offices and hosted a wine and cheese party to celebrate their success. Instead, it was a rout. The first Cubans had arrived two days before to help the MPLA; they shelled the invading forces, who fled in panic. P. W. Botha, now South Africa's state president but then defence minister, admitted later that he had been forced to send a South African frigate to rescue his artillerymen.

Meanwhile, with CIA encouragement, South Africa had sent an armoured column across Angola's southern border. By independence day it had sped 450 miles north and was within 125 miles of the capital. Each time it captured a town, it installed a joint Unita–FNLA government (although the two quickly fell to fighting between themselves).

But the CIA's open involvement in Angola caused a public outcry in the US, resulting in the passage of legislation (known as the Clark Amendment) prohibiting further aid to opposition movements in Angola. Without the promised US support, South Africa was forced to withdraw its forces. But as they left, they followed a scorched earth policy, destroying much of the infrastructure (including hundreds of bridges) in towns they had controlled. The total damage was more than £3,000 million, according to Angolan authorities. And in the decade since, South Africa has continued to support Unita.

To Lancaster House and beyond

Angola and Mozambique both joined the frontline states, which threw support behind Zanu and Zapu, the two liberation movements in Zimbabwe. Mozambique imposed the UN sanctions against Rhodesia (which Portugal had refused to honour). South Africa continued its economic and military backing for the Smith government, but pushed for some kind of internal settlement. This took shape in 1979 with a new 'Zimbabwe-Rhodesia' headed by Bishop Abel Muzorewa, but it received little international recognition. Finally in September

1979 Britain organized talks in Lancaster House in London, which by December resulted in agreement for free elections. In March 1980, Zanu won the elections overwhelmingly, and Robert Mugabe became prime minister in April. South Africa assumed Muzorewa would win, and provided financial and logistic support for his UANC party, but it won only three seats.

Zimbabwe, in turn, joined the front line states, which since then concentrated on supporting Swapo's fight to liberate Namibia – the last colony – and on ending apartheid in South Africa.

As the southern African map shows, Zimbabwe is at the heart of the region. Most of the roads and railways connecting the other majority-ruled states pass through Zimbabwe, making it the transport hub. It is also the most industrialized state in the region, outside South Africa itself. Thus the independence of Zimbabwe triggered a restructuring of economic and political relations throughout the region.

Economic liberation

The most important restructuring was the formation of the Southern African Development Coordination Conference (SADCC), an association of the majority-ruled states of the region. Political independence had not changed the fundamental economic relations of southern Africa – namely that South Africa is the dominant economic power. It is the main trading partner for many of the states, provides nearly 300,000 jobs for migrant workers, and is a focus for regional transport and communications. Two states (Lesotho and Swaziland) use the South African rand as their own currency, and three (Botswana, Lesotho, and Swaziland) are members of a customs union with the apartheid state. The majority-ruled states argued that they must break this economic dependence; that political independence must be complemented by 'economic liberation'.

During the fifteen years of UDI, precisely the period when most states in the region came to independence, Rhodesia was subject to sanctions by most states. Thus Rhodesia was like the hole in a doughnut, preventing direct contact between the independent states and forcing them to develop in isolation. With the independence of Zimbabwe, cooperation finally became possible. On 1 April 1980, even before Zimbabwe became formally independent, SADCC was formed. It was seen as the economic arm of the frontline states (FLS), but it also included the three non-members of the FLS: Lesotho, Malawi, and Swaziland.

SADCC is specifically *not* a common market, on the model of the EEC, but rather an attempt to coordinate transport, trade, and development. Many of the goods which member states buy from South Africa (or, for that matter, Europe) are already made locally; treating all of SADCC as a market makes production of a wide variety of goods viable. Electricity grids can be linked, making it possible to buy power from each other rather than from South Africa. Transport links can be improved, making it cheaper and faster to use SADCC ports rather than South African ones. It will be a long and slow process, but it is clearly possible to move towards economic integration and away from dependence on apartheid South Africa.

The initial motivation for SADCC was political, but it also made economic sense. As the nine states explained in their initial Lusaka Declaration, 'Towards Economic Liberation', their dependence on South Africa 'is not a natural phenomenon nor is it the result of a free market economy'. Rather, the nine states 'were deliberately incorporated – by metropolitan powers, colonial rulers, and large corporations – into the colonial and sub-colonial structures centring on the Republic of South Africa. The development of national economies as balanced units, let alone the welfare of the people of southern Africa, played no part in the economic integration strategy.'

But the historic dependence on South Africa dates back to early in the century, and it will take many years to end. And as I will argue later, South Africa is waging a war against its neighbours to ensure that their initiative fails.

Chapter Three

The addictive carrot

There are a vast array of economic links between South Africa and its neighbours. Many of these seem on the surface to be of benefit to the neighbours, particularly migrant labour and membership in the customs union.

The mines of the South African Rand were the focus of colonial development throughout the region in the first decades of this century. The neighbouring states provided much of the labour, and have continued to do so. Maputo (then Lourenço Marques) was developed as the main port. The mining town of Johannesburg became the industrial centre as well. One effect was that throughout the first half of the century, the neighbouring colonies developed fewer jobs and industries, remaining dependent on the South African connection.

South African mining capital also expanded into the neighbouring states. Today the giant Anglo American Corporation of South Africa dominates the economies of several countries. Anglo-controlled companies account for more than half of the entire value of the Johannesburg Stock Exchange – making it by far the largest company in South Africa itself. Internationally, it is now one of the biggest foreign investors in the United States. Through De Beers, it controls the world's diamond production and marketing; regionally De Beers owns or manages diamond mines in Botswana, Angola, Tanzania, Namibia, and South Africa itself – and markets the diamonds of the only other producer, Swaziland. It is active in other mining projects – as well as a wide variety of other industry including chemicals, engineering, and retailing – in Botswana, Zimbabwe, and Zambia. Anglo controls South African Breweries, which has a monopoly on bottled beer in South Africa and five of the neighbouring states (not unimportant, since beer is one of the largest industries in most developing countries).

Six other giant companies control another quarter of the value of the Johannesburg Stock Exchange (leaving less than one quarter not controlled by the seven monopoly groups – an incredible concentration of capital). South African companies, including Anglo, control one quarter of the entire capital stock of Zimbabwe – which itself is the most developed economy outside South Africa.

Rand zone and customs union

The three small states in the region – Botswana, Lesotho, and Swaziland (BLS) – were British protectorates. They were often administered from South Africa and at various times came close to being included in it. All three resisted, but the price was the loss of their best land to South Africa and almost total economic dependence.

In 1909, all three were included in a customs union with South Africa. This continued after independence, in a renegotiated form. Under the agreement, there is a free flow of goods (but not people) within the four member states, while there are high tariffs imposed on goods from outside. South Africa administers the system, collecting all tariffs on imported goods, and paying a share to the other three under a complex formula. The main gain to them is that they receive nearly £200 million each year, at little cost to themselves; this represents more than half of the government budget in Lesotho and Swaziland, and about one third in Botswana.

This is hardly money from heaven, however – it has four high, hidden costs. The most important one is that in all free trade zones, the free movement of goods ensures that the most developed members dominate. This means that South African companies totally dominate the economies of all three states, and new businesses are inevitably located in South Africa rather than in BLS. Recently, South Africa has been trying to encourage companies to start up in the bantustans, and actually gave grants for firms to move from B L S. Walking through the main shopping plazas in Gaborone (Botswana), Maseru (Lesotho), or Mbabane (Swaziland), one is struck by the fact that most of the shops are part of South African chains and the goods in the shops all come from across the border. Thus B L S import most of their consumer goods, machinery, and so on from South Africa, but sell relatively little in return. B L S have a trade deficit with South Africa that is four times as large as what they earn from the customs union. A study by the Botswana Ministry of Finance concluded that in 1979 B L S imports from South Africa accounted for 7 per cent of South Africa's manufacturing employment.

The second issue is in many ways related to South Africa's economic domination. South Africa sets the tariffs for all customs union members (without consulting them), and it has a highly protectionist policy of setting tariffs of 100 per cent or higher on goods which can be made locally. This has been a very effective spur to South African industrialization (and provides a strong argument for protectionism in newly industrializing countries). This is also directly related to South Africa's pariah status – there is substantial military pressure to produce strategic goods such as vehicles locally, so that they are not subject to sanctions. The problem is that, in common with other newly industrialized countries like India and Brazil, South Africa produces poorer quality but often more expensive goods. Only where labour costs are a major component do low wages counter-balance inefficiencies and make South African goods relatively less expensive. But high tariff rates mean that B L S are forced to buy South African goods, even when they are costly and tatty.

The third, and perhaps most obvious, point is that B L S do not have to be in the customs union to collect customs duties; they could easily collect customs duties themselves. Various studies suggest they would earn more money than they receive through the customs union – without pushing up the cost of living because they would be free to buy cheaper goods on the world market.

The final and most subtle point is that because customs union revenue is not perceived as a tax, it is often treated like a windfall. So, like Britain with its oil revenues, the money is spent on consumption rather than investment and industrial development.

Thus, the customs union is like a drug. Virtually all independent studies show that BLS would be better outside it, but they are hooked on the immediate revenue and consider it would be too much of a shock to pull out.

Because of the total South African dominance of their economies, both Lesotho and Swaziland actually use the South African rand as their own currency too. With diamonds to back it up, Botswana has issued its own currency, the pula. But because so much of Botswana trade is with South Africa, the international value of the pula must be kept close to that of the rand. Thus BLS have inherited South Africa's current economic crisis, and their currencies have collapsed along with the rand.

Migrant labour

Until the end of the 1970s, more than half of all miners in South Africa were migrants from neighbouring states. They worked on short-term contracts, typically twelve–fifteen months, and then returned home for six months or more. This system suited the mine owners, who could pay them relatively low wages and not have to provide housing or other facilities for families. The steady turnover of labour also made it hard for the miners to organize unions.

Three factors changed this pattern. First, a series of strikes in 1973 and 1974 pushed up wages throughout South Africa; mine wages rose faster than inflation for the first time in fifty years. This meant mine labour was not so cheap. Second, the growing unrest also brought pressure to provide more jobs for the unemployed inside South Africa. Third, the increasing modernization and mechanization of the mines has increased the demand for skilled workers, and thus for a permanent rather than a migrant workforce. As a result, the mines are rehiring from abroad only experienced men and are taking their new recruits from inside South Africa; thus the number of migrants from the neighbouring states is decreasing steadily, and could be negligible by the end of the century.

Nevertheless, migrant labour remains important, particularly for Lesotho. Nearly 150,000 people, more than half of the Basotho workforce, are in South Africa. They earn £150 million per year – the main source of income for the tiny mountain kingdom.

Five other countries have significant numbers of workers in South Africa, although combined they are still less than the Basotho. Perhaps 100,000 work in the mines and 40,000 on farms and as domestic servants, remitting over £100 million per year. Nearly one third of Botswana's working men are also in South Africa. For Swaziland it is 15 per cent, and for Malawi and Mozambique 5 per cent. Mozambique has 45,000 men in South Africa; it earns more from them than from its biggest export, cashew nuts.

Exports

South Africa's main exports are diamonds, gold, and other minerals. It is also an important exporter of food, chemicals, and machinery. But whereas the minerals are sold largely to the developed countries of Europe and the US and Japan, manufactured goods are sold mainly to Africa, and in particular to the neighbouring states. As I noted above, South Africa is a relatively high-cost producer of many industrial goods; the main export market for these is the neighbouring states because they are often not competitive on the world market. Because of the customs union, BLS have no choice but to buy. In order to sell to the other states of the region, South Africa uses a variety of tactics. Long-term credit and various discounts are common. South African companies in the neighbouring states sometimes buy from South Africa rather than on the world market, or from other states in the region, even if it would be cheaper.

But there are also other more subtle reasons, related to the fact that South Africa is the regional metropole. Most important, it *is* easier. All the neighbouring states are linked to South Africa by telex, telephone, regular flights, good roads, and railways. A telephone call to Johannesburg ensures that the goods or the spare part are there in a week, compared to three months for Europe. So saving money buying on the world market requires a degree of planning uncommon even among the multinational companies and international aid agencies. In one extreme case, the university teaching hospital in Lusaka ran out of antibiotics, even though the Zambia medical stores had them. So with a great public flourish, Prime Minister Jalumino Mundia sent a lorry to South Africa, because that was easier and faster than sorting out the local bureaucracy.

Partly it is racism – South Africa is seen as an extension of Europe and Europe is clearly 'better' than the third world. Thus South African goods are assumed to be better quality than those from India or Zimbabwe. This applies as much to white aid workers as to black bureaucrats.

I saw this happening in Mozambique. Much of the buying was still done by white Mozambicans, who found it easier to deal by telephone with Portuguese-speaking whites in South Africa – many of whom were old friends who had left Mozambique at independence. It was friendly, and the odd personal perk would usually be included in the package. Malawian exporters, for example, complained that the foreign currency shop in Maputo would only buy from South Africa and refused to buy high quality, luxury goods from Malawi. Sweden actually had to ban Mozambique from using its aid money to buy goods in South Africa. There was one instance in which a United Nations agency bought pipe in South Africa, despite objections from staff in Maputo that it would be cheaper to buy from Europe.

Equally important is that trading with South Africa can be used to wangle a trip there (which would be much less likely to Europe). That, in turn, means shopping for luxury goods not available in the neighbouring states, night life, and a holiday. Visiting black officials stay in 'international' (that is, integrated) hotels, so they are to some measure separated from apartheid. Furthermore, the South African vendor pays the bills, which is essential for bureaucrats from countries like Mozambique or Zambia where it is difficult to arrange foreign exchange.

Finally, there is corruption. One form is kickbacks. Poorly

paid officials who go to South Africa to collect goods sometimes come back with stereos or cars. Another is smuggling – drugs are sometimes smuggled into South Africa and wine or other luxury goods brought back in exchange. Zambia became a particular focus for such deals, and in late 1985 several former cabinet ministers were arrested for smuggling the drug Mandrax to South Africa.

Thus there is a substantial trade with South Africa. BLS, Zambia, Zimbabwe, and Malawi all import more from South Africa than from any other country. This is a vital support to South African manufacturing industry, which cannot sell elsewhere.

Energy and transport

South Africa is very short of energy resources, yet it has used these to create a dependency by the neighbouring countries. Despite the oil embargo, South Africa supplies all petroleum products to BLS, substantial amounts to Malawi, and some to Zimbabwe and Zambia as well. There is no economic reason to buy fuel from South Africa – the embargo has been successful enough to push the costs to South Africa to 50 per cent above the world market prices. These costs are passed on to those states which buy from South Africa. BLS pay an extra £15 million per year. But they have little choice. In chapters 1 and 12, I detail the lengths to which South Africa was prepared to go to prevent Zimbabwe, Lesotho, and Botswana from obtaining fuel elsewhere.

South Africa also supplies all Lesotho's electricity, and significant amounts to Botswana and Swaziland. It is contracted to buy substantial amounts of power from the Cahora Bassa Dam in Mozambique, as part of a deal organized by the Portuguese before Mozambican independence to link the two white minority-ruled states. One curious heritage of that deal is that the Mozambican capital, Maputo, is linked to the South African electricity grid and not to Cahora Bassa – the electricity goes first to South Africa and then back to Maputo.

Undoubtedly the most politically sensitive link is transport.

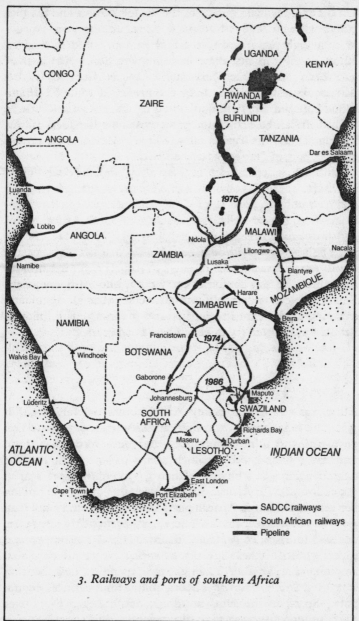

3. *Railways and ports of southern Africa*

Until 1974, the main outlets to the sea for Zambia and the then Rhodesia were the white-ruled Mozambique and Angola. Within eighteen months, there were four sudden changes: Rhodesia built its first direct rail link with South Africa (there had been an indirect link via Botswana since 1897, but Mozambique had always been the preferred route); Mozambique imposed sanctions and closed the border with Rhodesia; South African-backed Unita forces closed the Benguela railway in Angola; and the Tazara railway linking Zambia to Tanzania and the port of Dar es Salaam opened.

With the independence of Zimbabwe and the founding of SADCC, there was obvious economic pressure to use Angolan and Mozambican ports again. Independent of any political considerations, they were half the distance of South African ports, and thus much cheaper. Nevertheless, half of SADCC's imports and exports go through or to South Africa. This is because South Africa attacked the railways in Angola and Mozambique to ensure that they could not carry the traffic. Also, one of the South African monopoly groups, Old Mutual, dominates shipping in the entire region. It uses a variety of techniques, detailed in chapter 10, to keep cargo flowing south.

The £900-million connection

All things considered, South Africa comes out far ahead. It gives the neighbours £400 million per year in customs union payments and mine remittances, and buys more than £230 million of their goods – which seems a good deal. But the neighbouring states buy more than £1,300 million per year in goods from South Africa. Furthermore, they pay £150 million per year to use South African ports and railways, and more than £60 million per year for other services – particularly insurance, but also tourism, consultancy, maintenance of machinery, and so on. (Both of these are net balances, taking off the small amounts that South African tourists spend in neighbouring states and South Africa pays Mozambique for the use of Maputo port.) So when the sums are done, South Africa gains over £900 million per year from the neighbouring states. This is

vital to South Africa and to its industry. Thus economic dominance of the region is essential, and SADCC represents a serious
threat.

Table 2: Total regional deficit with South Africa
(based on Table 3 and text)

By country: trade, customs union, and migrants

Lesotho	£	43 million
Swaziland	129	
Botswana	233	
Zimbabwe	153	
Malawi	66	
Zambia	73	
Mozambique	1	
TOTAL	698	

Invisibles:

Ports and railways	150
Insurance, services	60
TOTAL	210

Total regional deficit with South Africa = £908 million

See pages 30–31 for Table 3.

Table 3: Economic dependence on South Africa

	LESOTHO	SWAZILAND	BOTSWANA
Trade:			
Main overall partner	RSA	RSA	RSA
Main source of imports	RSA	RSA	RSA
Imports from RSA	97% £250m	83% £275m	84% £342m
Exports to RSA	47% £12m	37% £72m*	17% £32m
Migrant workers:			
Number	135,000	14,000	35,000
Share of all formal sector workers	50%	15%	25%
Remittances	£150m	£5m	£11m
Customs union:			
% of government revenue	57%	67%	31%
Cash income	£45m	£69m	£66m
Overall deficit with RSA†	£43m	£129m	£233m
RSA supplies:			
Electricity	100%	77%	21%
Oil products	100%	100%	all
Food	most	some	some
Portion of foreign trade via RSA	all	half	most
Tourists			
Number and % of total	123,000 97%	47,000 59%	19,000 65%
RSA firms own, manage, or control:			
Mining	diamonds (closed)	coal, asbestos and diamonds	diamonds, coal and copper-nickel
Manufacturing	brewery and most other	brewery and most other	brewery and most non-agricultural
Retailing & distribution	most	most	most
Agriculture	wool marketing	pineapples, cotton and some timber	
Freight forwarding	all	all	all
Other dependence on RSA	rand zone	rand zone Main rivers rise in RSA	Some rivers rise in RSA Currency linked half to rand Rail transit traffic
RSA dependence on neighbour	Proposed Highland Water Scheme	Railway Transvaal –Richards Bay runs via Swaziland	Proposed soda-ash project

OTHER STATES:

Angola: Diamond mining controlled by South Africa; electricity supplied to Namibia from the Ruacana/Calueque hydro scheme; little trade or other commercial dealing with RSA.

Tanzania: Diamond mining controlled by South Africa; all other trade with RSA is banned.

NOTES:

Percentages are the share of the total, i.e. percentage of total exports, total imports, total number of wage workers, and total number of tourists (or visitors).

RSA: Republic of South Africa.

Table 3 (cont.)

	ZIMBABWE	MALAWI	ZAMBIA	MOZAMBIQUE
	RSA	RSA	UK	East Germany
	RSA	RSA	RSA	East Germany
	32% £263m	36% £67m	14% £76m	8% £39m
	17% £106m	6% £9m	1% £3m	2% £2m
	14,000	13,000	700	45,000
	2% £4m	4% £8m	(negligible)	5% £36m
	(not member)	(not member)	(not member)	(not member)
	£153m	£66m	£73m	£1m
	1%	none	none	28%
	little††	half	little	none
	none	luxury goods only	little	some vegetables
	three quarters	one third	half	none
	62,000 24%	2,500 40%	3,700 3%	none
	coal, nickel and some chrome	—	copper§	—
	beer, tobacco and many others	fertilizer	brewery, engineering	—
	largest firms	—	—	—
	sugar, timber, citrus	—	—	—
	most	most	most	most
	Trade agreement	some economic aid consultants and managers from RSA	consultants and mining supplies from RSA	Several rivers rise in RSA
	—	—	—	Cahora Bassa Dam contracted to supply 10% of RSA electricity needs; Some RSA coal and asbestos via Maputo

* 1982 figure. Now sharply reduced because of closure of RSA-owned fertilizer plant which provided bulk of exports to RSA.

† Taking account of trade and customs union and migrant labour payments, but not other invisibles such as ports, railways, insurance, and other services.

†† However, all oil products other than petrol and diesel are transported via South Africa.

§ Unofficially, through management and engineering links.

SOURCES:

Based on Hanlon, Joseph, *Beggar Your Neighbours*, CIIR and James Currey, to be published in 1986.

Most information is from 1982, the most recent year for which reasonably complete figures are available.

Volatile exchange rates mean that the £ figures will vary from one year to another.

Chapter Four

The 'total strategy' to defend apartheid

Driving north from Nelspruit in the eastern Transvaal of South Africa, I passed through lush and fertile valleys of irrigated banana and citrus. Suddenly as the car reached the crest of a hill, I saw a brown and barren valley packed with tiny houses spread out as far as the eye could see. There were few trees and no space for crops between the tightly packed hovels. The first valleys were white farmland, the next a 'homeland'; in South Africa the best land and the scarce water is for whites only.

During my five years as a journalist in Mozambique, I often visited rural villages; many were poor, but none were so impoverished as this. In the poorest Mozambican village, each family at least had access to enough land to grow their own food, and if not they could move somewhere else where there was land. Not in South Africa, where people are forced into these tiny bantustans or homelands.

I picked up a hitch-hiker, who told me he was on his way to see his wife and children. He had worked for fifteen years in a Johannesburg factory, but had no right to have his family there. So a few times a year he was allowed a long weekend to come more than 300 miles to this desolate place to visit them.

South African whites enjoy a living standard that would be impossible in Europe, with their servants, swimming pools, and privileged access to trains, beaches, and other facilities. But their luxury is built on the back of apartheid – on a system where black people do most of the work but reap few of the benefits, and have few rights. 'Reform' may remove some of the outward manifestations of apartheid, but white privilege is dependent on a fundamentally unequal society enforced by law.

Thus it is hardly surprising that many whites will fight to defend apartheid.

Nevertheless, there is a growing awareness within South Africa itself, not least by the big corporations, that the essential factor is the control of wealth and of the means of production. Some 'progressive' whites now argue quite strongly that the internationally objectionable aspects of apartheid are no longer useful, and indeed work against white interests. They see that privilege can be best maintained by dividing according to class rather than according to race.

South Africa's rapid economic growth was based on apartheid; the monopoly groups and mining houses earned their superprofits because of the extremely cheap labour provided by the apartheid system. But in the last decade, industry has modernized and cheap labour is less necessary. Instead, there is a shortage of skilled labour. At the same time, the five million whites do not provide a sufficient market for many industries. The answer is seen as creating black middle and skilled working classes, and granting this elite some political power. In particular, businessmen are anxious to end the identification of capitalism with apartheid. Many so-called 'progressive' whites, however, would only grant full status to a limited number of blacks, and vociferously oppose one-person one-vote. Gavin Relly, chairman of Anglo American and one of the most liberal businessmen, in 1985 stressed that he saw majority rule as unrealistic and unacceptable, and that it 'would have a devastating effect' on South Africa.

Thus the white community itself is divided between those who feel the need to defend traditional apartheid, and those who believe that white control can only be maintained by jettisoning some of those aspects of apartheid which are no longer useful.

Building apartheid

This book is about the neighbouring states rather than South Africa, so I will not go into too much detail about apartheid. More can be found in *The Apartheid Handbook* (Roger Omond, Penguin, 1985), *The Struggle for South Africa* (Rob Davies and others, Zed, 1984), and *South Africa in the 1980s* (Catholic Institute for International Relations, London, 1986). What is striking, however, is that apartheid as we know it is a very recent construct. In the first part of this century, South African mining and industry was built on cheap black labour. But before the Second World War, legally enforced racial discrimination was the norm in many parts of the world – in the southern United States and in British and Portuguese colonies, as well as in South Africa. What makes South Africa unique is that when this discrimination was being slowly reduced elsewhere, it was being strengthened and further institutionalized in South Africa.

When the Afrikaner National Party came to power in 1948, it introduced the formal concept of 'apartheid' in place of the simple segregation that had existed before. This called for the almost total separation of the four 'racial' groups: the 'whites', 'Coloureds' (mixed race and some Asian), 'Indians' (other Asians), and 'Africans'.* They were to have separate living areas, education systems, and so on. Not only was the 'African' majority to be discriminated against, it was to be denationalized; 'Africans' were to be made citizens of 'independent' homelands so that South Africa would be a white country. Even if they had been born in Soweto, 'Africans' suddenly became foreigners. It was rather as if all the people in London named Jones were informed they were now Welsh citizens with no right to a British passport and could only remain in England with special permission. There are now ten bantustans of which four have been given 'independence' by South Africa – an 'independence' recognized by no other country. Those four occupy one tenth of the land of South Africa (almost entirely poor quality land with no mineral or other resources) but are nominally assigned one sixth of the country's population.

* Because these racial divisions and the terminology that goes with them are imposed by the state, there is objection to the use of various terms. In general, all 'non-whites' consider themselves black, as in, for example, Black Consciousness, a movement that includes people the state classifies into three separate groups. Black is used in that sense throughout this book, to mean all 'non-white' people. The state now uses 'black' to refer only to the majority it once called 'natives' and then 'Bantu'; it does not use 'African' for this group because in the Afrikaans language 'Afrikaner' simply means African, and Afrikaners are clearly 'white'. To avoid confusion over the word black, when forced to discuss the three subject race groups, we will refer to them as 'Coloured', 'Indian', and 'African' – always in quotation marks.

In the early 1950s the National government introduced its basic apartheid legislation. The 1950 Group Areas Act reserved residential and business areas for different racial groups, leading to largescale removals and ending what residential integration still existed. The same year the Immorality Amendment Act banned inter-racial sex. 'Coloureds' lost their vote. Pass laws were strengthened. Job reservation was enforced to reserve many skilled jobs for whites, while black unions were sharply restricted (this had the side effect of forcing down 'African' wages).

Inevitably there was resistance. In 1955 the Freedom Charter was approved at a mass 'Congress of the People'. This was followed by a protracted campaign against the extension of the pass laws. The government responded with legal action, and in 1956 it charged 156 leaders of the Congress Alliance with treason – all were acquitted after a five-year trial. A turning point was probably the Sharpeville massacre of 21 March 1960, when police opened fire and killed sixty-nine demonstrators. This was followed then by the declaration of a state of emergency and the banning of the two main anti-apartheid organizations, the African National Congress (ANC) and the Pan Africanist Congress (PAC).

The Treason Trial may not have brought convictions, but it was successful in driving many leaders into exile and in keeping others out of action for nearly five years. The banning of the ANC and PAC effectively brought to a temporary end legal internal protest and resistance to the implementation of apartheid.

The ANC and PAC launched sabotage campaigns inside South Africa, but they were quickly crushed by the security forces. Much of the ANC's underground leadership was caught at Rivonia in 1963. The banning of legal protest, the loss of the leadership to jail or exile, and the introduction of a series of ever stronger security laws effectively suppressed mass action for the next decade.

Independence outside boosts the struggle inside

In the 1960s, the problems were more from outside than inside. Apartheid was becoming internationally unacceptable, and South Africa had to leave the Commonwealth in 1961. More important, the tide of decolonization and majority rule was rolling south; Tanzania became independent in 1961, followed by Malawi and Zambia in 1964. Botswana and Lesotho came to independence in 1966, and Swaziland in 1968, but they were less a threat because of their close economic links and because all three were still surrounded by white rule. Portugal and Ian Smith's Rhodesia held out; they served as buffer states of white rule protecting apartheid. It was not a military cordon keeping guerrillas away from South Africa, but more of a psychological cordon – the four countries with the largest white populations (Rhodesia, Angola, Mozambique, and South Africa) were cooperating to maintain white rule.

Thus the 1974 Portuguese coup, and independence in Mozambique and Angola the following year, came as a bitter shock. Again it was political and psychological, because both new states were committed to multiracialism and socialism. If they were allowed to succeed, it would destroy the entire ideological underpinnings of apartheid. A wave of black strikes had begun in 1973 and the independence of Mozambique and Angola gave a particular boost to those struggling inside South Africa. The new movement was Black Consciousness, and nine of its leaders were jailed for an illegal rally to celebrate the peaceful installation of the Frelimo government in Mozambique. In June 1976 the Soweto uprising marked a new phase of the struggle, and of police repression; in September 1977 Black Consciousness leader Steve Biko was killed in police custody, provoking a worldwide outcry. In November the United Nations Security Council approved a mandatory arms embargo.

The government response to the changes inside and outside South Africa was confused. Prime Minister B. J. Vorster and his Bureau of State Security (BOSS) had orchestrated a 'detente' campaign to try to win black allies. South Africa had established diplomatic relations with Malawi in 1966 but had made no progress with other majority-ruled states until the short-lived detente exercise, when Vorster went to the Ivory Coast and Liberia and met with Zambia's President Kenneth Kaunda. But the military and the then defence minister, P. W. Botha, counselled a hard line. Botha tried to invade Mozambique in September 1974 to support a settler uprising, hoping for a white U D I in Mozambique similar to the one in Rhodesia; but Vorster was opposed and BOSS disabled the armoured column as it waited at the border town of Komatipoort. But the next year there was consensus, and P. W. Botha was allowed to invade Angola – only to have to withdraw with his tail between his legs.

Meanwhile, the economy was in trouble. Falling gold prices pulled the economy into recession from 1974 to 1978, while the Soweto uprising, the Biko killing, and the wave of bannings of organizations and individuals provoked a second wave of disinvestment (the first had been after Sharpeville).

The 'total strategy'

The military offered the solution white South Africa craved. P. W. Botha became head of the National Party and prime minister in 1978. His explanation of the crisis had been set out in the 1977 Defence White Paper. South Africa faced a 'total Marxist onslaught' – a Moscow-orchestrated plot to overthrow white rule. The onslaught involved political, diplomatic, and economic action as well as military effort; criticism of apartheid and calls for sanctions were claimed to be communist inspired. According to Defence Minister Magnus Malan, even 'the western powers make themselves available as handymen of the communists' when they oppose apartheid. 'Like creeping lava and suffocating gas,' warned Foreign Minister Pik Botha, 'the menacing hegemony of Russia is spreading over this planet.' This view continues until now. A commentary on the state-controlled radio on 15 June 1985 responded to the continuing township uprising and calls for sanctions by declaring that the Soviet Union was 'instigating discontent among the country's black people through the exploitation of real and trumped-up grievances' and that the disinvestment campaign had been 'cleverly planned' by the KGB.

The answer to the 'total onslaught' had to be the 'total national strategy' – which involved all sectors of society in a military-led defence of white rule. Apartheid needed to be streamlined, and the most objectionable features removed; 'Coloureds' and 'Indians' would be given some political rights, the growth of a black middle class encouraged, and petty apartheid restrictions would be removed. The military itself was to be strengthened, and the defence budget doubled in the next five years. The whole structure of government was subtly changed; the white parliament and the ordinary government ministries lost power, and a military-dominated State Security Council became the main decision-making body. Big business, which until then had been ostracized from the corridors of political power, was to have a role in the 'total strategy'.

The total strategy may have been moderately reformist inside, but it was hard outside. The 1977 Defence White Paper stressed the need to 'maintain a solid military balance relative to neighbouring states'. It also called for 'economic action' and 'action in relation to transport services, distribution, and tele-communications' to push 'political and economic collaboration among the states of southern Africa'.

The idea was to form a Constellation of States (Consas) which would include South Africa, the 'independent' bantustans, Namibia, Zimbabwe-Rhodesia under Bishop Abel Muzorewa, the three majority-ruled states that were not in the frontline states (Malawi, Lesotho, and Swaziland) and probably Botswana and Zambia. It was seen as an explicitly anti-communist grouping, and was predicated on the assumption that the neighbouring states felt that they all faced a common Marxist threat.

Consas collapses

The Bothas' dream of Consas was naive, because it was built on two false assumptions: first that Muzorewa would win an election in Zimbabwe, and second that the majority-ruled neighbours shared the fear of a communist onslaught.

Clearly Zimbabwe was the keystone to any regional grouping. The frontline states (FLS) and the Bothas each unveiled their plans in 1979 on the assumption that their side would win in Zimbabwe. The first shock to Pretoria was the massive Zanu victory in Zimbabwe on 4 March 1980. On 1 April Robert Mugabe took Zimbabwe into the FLS and SADCC rather than Consas. The second shock was when all three other non-FLS members also joined SADCC. Clearly apartheid was seen as more evil than socialism.

Lesotho, although totally surrounded by South Africa, had been moving steadily away from it politically; for example, in 1978, Lesotho hosted an UN anti-apartheid seminar and opened warm relations with Mozambique. So important figures in the Lesotho government were already retreating from Pretoria's political grasp. The other two states, however, had very conservative rulers who had maintained links with South Africa. Nevertheless, they too were drifting away. Malawi, the only majority-ruled state in Africa to have diplomatic links with Pretoria, had sharply cut the number of migrant miners going to South Africa, reduced its purchases from South Africa (from 41 per cent of total imports in 1979 to 32 per cent in 1981), and was quietly building better links with its neighbours.

Swaziland, too, was moving away; it gave tacit agreement for ANC guerrillas to pass from Mozambique through Swaziland to South Africa, and became more critical of apartheid. On 6 April 1981 it hosted a meeting of the heads of Mozambique, Botswana, and Lesotho which issued a communiqué denouncing 'attempts by South Africa to destabilize her neighbouring black-ruled states'. Such words had not been heard from Swaziland before – or since. Swaziland also announced a policy of reducing economic dependence on South Africa. It began a major hydroelectricity scheme and built an earth station for satellite telecommunications, both explicitly to replace services bought from South Africa.

Thus none of the neighbouring states were willing to be seen consorting with apartheid and the bantustans, and all supported delinking. SADCC was a severe blow to South Africa because it certified the political isolation of the apartheid state in southern Africa. It was also an economic blow, because of its explicit commitment to reduce economic links with South Africa.

Meanwhile, the apartheid state was hit by two other serious blows. South Africa has no oil and was importing most of its needs from Iran; the overthrow of the Shah suddenly turned off that tap, and in early 1980 South Africa nearly ran out of oil. Then on 1 June 1980 the ANC bombed the two Sasol plants which make oil from coal, and also bombed a refinery. It marked the beginning of serious ANC sabotage actions inside South Africa, and was particularly traumatic because it damaged heavily guarded oil facilities at the height of the oil crisis. By late 1980, white South Africa felt under siege.

Chapter Five

Regional power

P. W. Botha had pinned his regional hopes on Consas, which was shot down in flames. This underlined the increasing pressure on South Africa's white leadership from both inside and outside. That, in turn, made it all the more essential to find ways to dominate the region. To see why, it is necessary to look at the neighbouring states through the eyes of the apartheid leadership, in the context of what General Malan calls South Africa's four 'power bases': security, social/psychological, economic, and diplomatic.

● The *security* aspect is directly linked to the use of neighbouring states by the liberation movements. ANC, PAC, and Swapo are all recognized by the Organization of African Unity; they have observer status at some SADCC meetings and political representatives in most of the neighbouring capitals. ANC (and to a lesser extent PAC) guerrillas were infiltrating into South Africa from the neighbouring states, and Swapo does have bases in Angola. The importance of this infiltration is vastly exaggerated; the unrest in South Africa's townships is primarily a direct response to apartheid. But its stress on guerrillas allows the Pretoria government to argue that the 'natives' really are happy and that the only problem is communist terrorists sent to South Africa by Moscow. In part, it is propaganda for internal purposes, to justify the expanding military budget and ever stronger security laws. Nevertheless, like its misperceptions about Consas, the military also seems to genuinely believe that the threat is outside; at least some in the military really do believe that blacks are not bright enough to plan a sabotage campaign, and that there must be white communist masters somewhere. Thus they believe they can fight the war outside South Africa rather than inside.

The South African Defence Forces (SADF) have built strong links with Israel and have obtained important military hardware as well as strategic advice. In particular, Pretoria wants to do with the ANC what Israel is trying to do with the Palestine Liberation Organization (PLO) – pushing it out of all neighbouring states. This involves attacks on ANC members in neighbouring states, not only on those South Africa claims are guerrillas, but also official and political representatives. Finally there is Israeli-style retaliation for major ANC sabotage raids, usually involving an attack on a neighbouring state.

South Africa usually says that its major security demand is that neighbouring states should not be used as 'springboards' for guerrilla attacks inside South Africa. In practice, however, Pretoria hopes to prevent any ANC, PAC, or Swapo presence.

Although direct air force and commando attacks are sometimes used, the main military tactic is destabilization. This is a mix of economic and military pressure, usually covert, designed – as the word implies – to create instability. Sometimes it is a means to extract concessions from the neighbouring states, such as expulsion of the ANC (but more often economic, see below). But it is important to remember that chaos is an end in itself, and not necessarily a means to some more subtle goal. A country in chaos has less time and resources to worry about the overthrow of apartheid. (Destabilization is discussed in more detail in the next chapter.)

● The *social/psychological* 'power base' of apartheid is threatened by the neighbouring states because they represent a fundamental danger to its ideological underpinnings. If the region has prosperous, multiracial, socialist states, then Anglo's Gavin Relly can no longer argue that majority rule would have a 'devastating effect' in South Africa. Thus chaos in the neighbouring states allows Pretoria to point out that the alternatives to apartheid are worse. An acceptable alternative is to have majority-ruled states subservient, because it again allows the claim that white rule is necessary. Destabilization is ideal for enforcing one or the other.

P. W. Botha went to great lengths in 1985 to prevent South Africans from talking to or reading about ANC President Oliver Tambo. He reinforced the ban on press interviews with Tambo, and ordered the confiscation of passports from people who said they were going to Lusaka to talk to the ANC. But this only emphasized how frightened the leadership is that South Africans of all races will learn that there are viable alternatives to apartheid. The social/psychological power base is clearly very fragile.

● The *economic* role of the neighbouring states is two-fold. The obvious one is that it is a source of tens of thousands of jobs in South Africa and a net flow of £900 million per year to South Africa. As the depression worsens and South Africa faces sanctions and disinvestment, that market becomes increasingly important. But economic power has another, probably more important, role in the region. Deon Geldenhuys of Rand Afrikaans University pointed out that it is 'a common phenomenon in international relations that states use their economic ties with others for non-economic political and military/security purposes'. In his article in the South African journal *ISSUP Strategic Review* (January 1981), he argued that South Africa had a variety of 'economic levers' that it could apply to the neighbours. And he stressed that 'South Africa should endeavour to keep black states as economically dependent as possible, thereby circumscribing their freedom of economic, political and also military action *vis-à-vis* South Africa'; in particular, if they became less dependent, they might 'adopt an even more assertive and militant policy towards South Africa since the latter's means of retaliation would have been curtailed'.

Thus it is in South Africa's regional security interest to keep the neighbours dependent. Since, as repeatedly noted here, that dependence is not 'natural' or based on cheaper or better goods and services, military action and economic sabotage are needed to enforce that dependence.

● The fourth 'power base' is the *diplomatic* one. South Africa's international links are essential for its survival. It is dependent on capital and technology from the west, both for industrial development and for building up its war machine. But they are also politically and psychologically vital; precisely because whites see themselves as the bastion of western civilization in a hostile black land, so they need to retain their contact with other white countries. It is this which makes social sanctions like the sport and cultural boycotts so painful.

Thus white South Africa is always searching for ways to rebuild its links with Europe. Prime Minister Vorster argued that the road to Europe goes through Africa. This was one reason for his detente exercise – to gain political acceptance within a few African states, and to parlay this into readmission to polite society. In a broad sense this is still the view in Pretoria, and in 1984 it proved correct, when South Africa bludgeoned Mozambique into signing the Nkomati Accord (discussed in detail in chapter 14). South Africa had been pressing its neighbours for years to sign such non-aggression pacts, and until then all had refused. (Except Swaziland, which had agreed one secretly two years before.) Thus the signing in a blaze of publicity was a major diplomatic coup, and P. W. Botha was able to make an official tour of Europe only three months later. P. W. Botha himself described the tour as the end of South Africa's 'years in the desert', while the South African press stated that the trip was possible only because the accord had given Pretoria a new credibility.

This is linked to the previous ideological point. South Africa has always played on the latent racialism in western Europe and the United States, and their underlying belief that blacks cannot rule themselves. P. W. Botha talks of South Africa bringing 'salvation' to the neighbouring states, and of the west preventing this by its actions against apartheid. Thus Pretoria needs chaos or subservience next door to justify whatever remaining position it has in world forums. By contrast, successful majority-ruled states show that alternatives are possible and that apartheid does not represent 'salvation'. (There is also a danger inside South Africa that majority-ruled states serve as a model and thus provide a spur to the struggle.)

Regional power

The white leadership in Pretoria concluded that it was essential to have what it called regional hegemony – the economic and military dominance of the region – to ensure that its four 'power bases' remained intact. Prior to 1975, the white rulers in the neighbouring states had accepted South African hegemony. By 1980, all the neighbouring states explicitly rejected it. Thus the past six years have seen a war for the control of southern Africa – will the majority-ruled states determine their own destinies, or will they be dominated by South Africa?

Attacks on the neighbouring states produced some international protests, and Pretoria could no longer claim the right to hegemony in the way it could in the days of regional white rule. Yet the total strategy and the defence of apartheid power bases demanded regional dominance. A political justification for regional dominance only coalesced in 1984, when South Africa declared itself a 'regional power'. In a series of speeches Pik Botha and P. W. Botha referred to this as a kind of Monroe Doctrine for southern Africa, referring to the claim in 1823 by the US President James Monroe that the US had the right to dominate Latin America and that Europe should not interfere. They also argued that South Africa had a right to the same kind of hegemony over the region as the USSR had over eastern Europe.

South Africa's version of this concept accepts that it is not in the same league as the US or USSR. Rather it is a *regional* power in that it sits between the superpowers – the US and USSR – and the smaller states of the region. Thus the Bothas now accept that both the US and USSR have 'justifiable global interests' in the region, but at the same time declare that the superpowers cannot do anything that 'would endanger South Africa's essential regional interests'.

Internally, the superpowers have no right to interfere in South Africa's 'value system and social structure' – in other words, they cannot attack apartheid. Regionally, South Africa reserves the right to intervene in neighbouring states, in P. W. Botha's words, to prevent 'instability' or if the benefit 'of superpower assistance fails to materialize'. This curious latter claim seems aimed at permitting intervention in states aided by the socialist bloc. Furthermore, the Cubans must withdraw from Angola: 'They must go. Fair or not, that's it. We are the regional power. It is our region,' declared Foreign Minister Pik Botha. Finally, the superpowers should not support the SADCC goal of reducing economic links with South Africa.

So far, only the United States has backed white South Africa's brazen claim to be king of southern Africa. The Reagan administration has, in any case, always argued it cannot interfere with apartheid, wanted the Cubans out, and opposed SADCC aims to delink.

Thus Pretoria is forced into actions which will justify its claim to be a regional power. As well as the obvious need for continued economic and military dominance, South Africa needs to establish some regional legitimacy. In other words, the neighbouring states must be forced to acknowledge that South Africa is a regional power. This can be seen in five kinds of demands.

● That neighbouring states should sign non-aggression pacts with South Africa. (So far Swaziland and Mozambique have done so; Botswana and Lesotho have resisted, despite extreme pressure.) The point of signing an accord is not to stop aggression, but rather that it gives international diplomatic standing to Pretoria's claims. P. W. Botha's invitations to visit Europe after the public signing of the Nkomati Accord with Mozambique shows that this is the case.

● That neighbouring states should give South Africa the maximum possible diplomatic recognition. Pretoria would dearly like more embassies in the neighbouring states, but the only one is still in Malawi, opened two decades ago. Pretoria accepts that no majority-ruled state could hold its head up at the OAU if it allowed an embassy, thus it considered the opening of a trade mission in Swaziland in 1985 as a major success. With little possibility of more such missions, the South Africans often use mundane issues to force neighbouring states to meet it at ministerial level, for example to deal with minor border or transport issues. Elsewhere in the world, such matters would be settled by high-level civil servants, but Pretoria wants the international recognition of its government ministers meeting neighbouring black ministers. This was a central point in the negotiations with Zimbabwe over blocked oil supplies discussed in chapter 1. This may seem arcane to many people, but Pretoria is fighting international isolation; if not even ministers from neighbouring states will talk to it, then South Africa can hardly expect international acceptance for its claims to be a regional power.

● That neighbouring states should allow South African soldiers on their soil, even if only for disaster relief. This reinforces South Africa's claim to be a regional policeman. Swaziland did allow South African troops in to help with flood relief. Mozambique has been under strong pressure to do so as part of the Nkomati non-aggression pact, for example to guard South African technicians, to guard the Cahora Bassa power line, and even to do agricultural development work. But Maputo has consistently refused. South Africa also tries to present itself as a peacekeeper or 'mediator' between neighbouring states and anti-government groups that Pretoria actually controls.

● That tacit recognition be given to apartheid structures. This usually involves trying to force the neighbouring states to negotiate directly with, or at least sit in joint meetings with, the so-called 'independent' bantustans. So far, all the neighbouring states have religiously refused to do so.

● That, in the words of Deon Geldenhuys, 'black states in southern Africa display some moderation in expressing their customary criticism' of apartheid. He admits that 'it simply cannot be expected of OAU member states to refrain from denouncing apartheid; at issue is the manner in which it is done'. This remains a major concern. After the raid on Lesotho described in chapter 1, Pretoria tried to force Lesotho to sign a non-aggression pact. The then foreign minister, Evaristus Sekhonyana, told me that one clause in the proposed accord forbade unfriendly acts. 'I asked them: "Suppose the university students just hold a meeting and criticize apartheid. Would you consider that an unfriendly act?" And they said yes. They wanted us to crack down internally on criticism of apartheid.'

Chapter Six

Destabilization

The economic and military methods most commonly used by South Africa against the neighbouring states are normally grouped together under the heading of 'destabilization'. It is hard to define explicitly or pin down, Deon Geldenhuys points out, because 'hardly any state would ever admit it was engaged in destabilization activities against another'. And he notes that 'destabilization activities usually take a covert form, with the destabilizer taking care to cover his tracks to and from the scene of the crime'.

Geldenhuys goes on to argue that 'the destabilizer's objective is an avowedly political one. Essentially, he wishes to promote (or force) profound political changes in the target state ... At the very least, the destabilizer demands a fundamental shift or reorientation in the target state's policy *vis-à-vis* the destabilizer.' Thus 'the destabilizer is not interested in actions which the target state would consider to be mere irritants or annoyances'.

Then he takes the crucial step, and argues that since the neighbours are trying to end apartheid and white rule, they are demanding just such a fundamental shift in South Africa – in other words, the neighbours are destabilizing it. Furthermore, 'black states' political and moral support for the so-called liberation movements, and their clamour for sanctions against South Africa and for its international isolation, are part of a concerted campaign to destabilize the country'. This is a crucial point – *political* (as distinct from military) support for the ANC, and mere public *calls* for sanctions, as in the UN, are hostile acts. And if South Africa is being destabilized, it has a clear right to destabilize in return. In other words, *South Africa has a right to destabilize its neighbours because they oppose apartheid.*

Deon Geldenhuys became an associate professor of political science at Rand Afrikaans University in Johannesburg in 1982. He could be considered a Machiavelli of destabilization, because he has produced a shoal of papers analysing the concept and showing how to carry it out, while maintaining a certain academic distance. For example, in one prescription for destabilizing the neighbours he admits in passing that the 'most reliable way of ... creating an acceptable regional environment' is through 'drastic political reform in South Africa'. After tacitly admitting the impossibility of reform, he spends seven pages listing ways to pummel the neighbouring states, only to argue at the end of the paper that to produce such a list of actions 'is decidedly not to suggest or advocate their use. It is merely a legitimate academic exercise.'

Whatever his view of these 'academic exercises', others were listening. Much of the rest of this book details how suggestions by Geldenhuys and others were carried out. But when reading the later chapters, it is useful to remember that I am not quoting from secret military documents. The recipe for destabilization was contained in papers by Geldenhuys and others that had been openly published in academic journals *before* most of the actions reported here took place.

In one paper, published by the South Africa Forum as a 'Position Paper' in September 1982, he stresses the importance of the destabilizer attacking 'the target state's political, economic, and military vulnerabilities'. He points to the opportunities 'to lend support to [receptive] disaffected groups'. Such 'military support can assume more or less covert forms: providing arms and equipment, recruiting and arming mercenaries, sending own military personnel as advisors or as combatants', and setting up radio stations for the rebels. (This was already being done in Mozambique, Angola, Lesotho, and Zimbabwe, and the military did not need his help to point to this obvious method.)

Another suggestion is to cut food supplies to the neighbouring states. 'The objective could be to cause serious hardship to the population, who would in turn direct their frustration and fury at the target's regime.' (This was done in Mozambique, with the involvement of military support mentioned above, creating a famine; food supplies to Zambia and Lesotho have also been disrupted.)

The most important of Geldenhuys's 'academic exercises' was a study of economic rather than military actions that could be taken against the neighbours. It was commissioned by the Institute of Strategic Studies of the University of Pretoria (ISSUP) – an institution with the closest links to the military. And it was published in January 1981, before Pretoria launched its destabilization policy in earnest. In the following two years, virtually all his recommendations were carried out. They included:

● Limiting the use of South African railways, for example by 'manipulating the availability of railway wagons'. (Done to Zimbabwe, Botswana, Lesotho, and Zambia.)

● Restrictions on migrant labour. (Done to Zimbabwe; Mozambique and Lesotho threatened.)

● Border closures or restrictions. (Done to all immediate neighbours: Lesotho, Swaziland, Zimbabwe, Botswana, and Mozambique.)

● Curbing imports from neighbouring states. (Done to Zimbabwe and Swaziland.)

● 'Regulating the export of goods to black states', especially 'food and oil'. (Done to Botswana, Lesotho, Malawi, Mozambique, Zambia, and Zimbabwe.)

● Cutting electricity supplies. (Done to Lesotho and Mozambique.)

● Restricting South African tourists. (Done to Lesotho and Swaziland.)

● Violating the customs union agreement. (Done to all three other members: Botswana, Lesotho, and Swaziland.)

Buffer against sanctions

Thus destabilization is primarily economic, and even military action often has economic ends. The overall goal of destabilization is to assert and maintain regional dominance. Destabilization also has a number of specific aims, of which the most important relate to sanctions. This is because sanctions are seen as the most serious threat to white rule.

Deon Geldenhuys, in his key ISSUP paper, said that a goal of destabilization must be to force the neighbouring states to 'not support calls for mandatory trade sanctions against South Africa'. And he argued that 'the stronger their economic ties with South Africa, perhaps the lesser the chances of their supporting sanctions. *Black states could, in other words, shield South Africa from mandatory sanctions.*' (Emphasis added.) The neighbouring states should be a buffer against sanctions – just as Pretoria hopes to make them a barrier against liberation movements, and two decades ago saw them as a buffer against majority rule.

This is to be done by keeping the neighbours economically dependent on South Africa – for goods, services, and jobs. Thus it will be possible to argue that sanctions will hurt the neighbouring states, either directly or via South African retaliation. The two most sensitive points are transport and migrant labour, and when the sanctions issue came to the fore in 1985 high South African officials threatened to cut off both. Sometimes it was stated quite explicitly – if you impose sanctions we will send miners home in retaliation. Sometimes it was indirect – if the west cuts mineral imports there will be less need for miners, and naturally we will send the foreigners home first. Similar comments have been made about rail and port traffic, and about trade, particularly with the three customs union states (Botswana, Lesotho, and Swaziland).

The problem for South Africa with this argument is that it only works so long as the neighbouring states remain dependent, and as we noted in chapter 3 they do not want or need to be. The clearest example is with transport, and was illustrated in the opening chapter – the neighbouring states only use South African ports and railways because South Africa has blown up their own and thus they have no choice.

And SADCC becomes a major target of destabilization. If SADCC succeeded in reducing dependence on South Africa, then Pretoria could no longer claim that sanctions would hurt the neighbours.

Pretoria would like at least one or two neighbouring states to make explicit anti-sanctions declarations, but this is unlikely to happen. The next best thing is to argue that the neighbouring states are so economically dependent on it that sanctions will hurt, but that they cannot say so for fear of offending other black states.

This is, in reality, a curious circular argument: South Africa is destabilizing its neighbours and sanctions could force it to mend its ways, but destabilization has made the neighbours economically dependent on South Africa, thus sanctions should not be imposed because they will hurt the victim more than the aggressor.

The British foreign office and 'liberal' white politicians inside South Africa actually use this argument against sanctions. In fact, it is not true, as is shown later; it is also firmly refuted by the neighbouring states themselves. Nevertheless, South Africa's economic power in the region serves a useful function in its international relations.

Contradictions

So far, I have treated white South Africa as a rather unified object. In practice, however, big and small business, diplomats, and the military all have very different interests.

For example, economic dominance of the region is important for two reasons – to provide £900 million per year, and to give Pretoria political power over the neighbouring states. But these are in conflict – border closures, transport disruptions, and so on all make it harder to do business with the neighbouring states, and encourage them to follow the SADCC goals of delinking. Furthermore, 'economic levers' are really sanctions by another name, and if South Africa is seen to be using sanctions against its neighbours, that strengthens the arguments of those who want to impose sanctions against South Africa.

Similarly, destabilization disrupts neighbouring economies, making it hard for businesses to export to them. For example, in Mozambique dissidents controlled by the South African military have kidnapped technicians working for South African companies.

In part, this reflects sharp differences in perception. The right wing, strongly represented in the military, claims that it is never possible to trust the Marxists. To them, the only possibility is to keep them in chaos or even overthrow them. Yet businesses are anxious to sell to the Marxist states. Furthermore, a diplomatic goal is to make the neighbouring states more cooperative and willing to deal with Pretoria – which is less likely if the military is trying to overthrow the government. One of the more extreme examples of differing perception was the military in a Defence White Paper dismissing Zambia's President Kenneth Kaunda as an irredeemable Marxist just as P. W. Botha was trying to arrange talks with him.

Another conflict between the defence and foreign ministries is over the effect of destabilization on South Africa's international image. When Pik Botha is trying to put over an image of South Africa as peacemaker, it does not help him when the air force bombs a neighbouring state.

Nevertheless, it is also important not to push these conflicts too far. Both business and diplomats see destabilization as a useful weapon, and support the 'thump and talk' approach of the total strategy. One of the concessions that South Africa extracted from Mozambique, for example, was to make the country more open to South African business. Similarly, the diplomats see destabilization as a useful way to soften up the neighbours, and make them more willing to talk. The contradictions, then, are not over broad strategy, but over when to switch from sjambok to carrot.

Chapter Seven

Political intervention

South Africa has regularly intervened in its neighbours' political affairs. On 5 January 1984 at a government guesthouse in Pretoria, the South African foreign minister and his deputy, Pik Botha and Louis Nel, met various Lesotho opposition leaders, including a former foreign minister of Lesotho, C. D. Molapo. (Molapo had already been accused of having secret South African links – see chapter 1.) Pik Botha encouraged them to form an opposition party, and he promised them funds, so they set up the Basuto Democratic Alliance (BDA).

Two things were striking about the formation of the BDA. The first was how completely the participants in the meeting misjudged the mood in Lesotho. The BDA was a fiasco which drew no local support. Leabua Jonathan may not have been popular in Lesotho, but Pik Botha was even less popular. Too many Basotho have first-hand experience of apartheid, particularly as miners. The second striking factor was the brazenness of it. We know about the Pretoria luncheon because both Basotho and South African participants were happy to talk to the press about the role of Botha and Nel in forming an opposition party in another country. The South African response was simply to remind the press that it was South Africa that had put Jonathan in power in 1965 and kept him there in 1970.

In Lesotho's 1965 pre-independence elections, the manifesto of Chief Leabua Jonathan's Basutoland National Party (BNP) called for collaboration with South Africa. In turn, South Africa provided the BNP with campaign funds, a helicopter, and exclusive access to Basotho miners in South Africa. The BNP won by a narrow margin.

In the 1970 elections the BNP platform again stressed the importance of cooperation with South Africa. The electorate disagreed, and the BNP was overwhelmingly defeated by the Basutoland Congress Party (BCP). So, with South African help, Jonathan simply abrogated the election and stayed in power. But he recognized the will of the electorate, and in the next two years turned away from Pretoria. He called on other African states not to have links with South Africa, and asked for foreign aid to help Lesotho delink.

South Africa was not pleased, and in 1972 tried unsuccessfully to overthrow him. Another South African-backed coup attempt failed in 1974; the BCP leader Ntsu Mokhehle fled to South Africa, where he was allowed to stay. The South Africans later provided him with a military force, the Lesotho Liberation Army (LLA), to try again.

Support for Muzorewa

South Africa was also active in Zimbabwe. In the pre-independence election in March 1980, it threw its support behind Bishop Abel Muzorewa and his UANC. Pretoria provided substantial amounts of money, and worked with the Rhodesian security service to organize the campaign. A high-security official, Geoffrey Price, was involved in the Muzorewa campaign. One government official told me: 'Price wrote Muzorewa's speeches; he hired the buses and helicopters, organized the rallies, and even arranged the Cokes. But it was all with South African money and according to South African instructions.'

In the event, Pretoria again backed the wrong side. The two groups that had won the liberation war also won nearly all eighty seats: Robert Mugabe's Zanu-PF won fifty-seven seats, Joshua Nkomo's Zapu took twenty. The Bishop won just three.

Widening the Zanu–Zapu split

When political intervention failed, South Africa resorted to dirty tricks. Undoubtedly its most successful manoeuvre widened the divisions between Zanu and Zapu. There were always tensions between the two, rooted in ethnic, personal, and political difference. Even during the liberation war when they joined into the Patriotic Front, Zanu and Zapu still fought as separate armies.

After independence, Robert Mugabe stressed a policy of reconciliation – between Zanu and Zapu, and between black and white. But it was always tenuous, because of the long-standing differences. Thus an important South African target was to widen those divisions and prevent that reconciliation. The one single event that did most to split Zanu and Zapu was the disclosure that Zapu members had cached arms rather than turning them into the central armoury. The disclosure provoked the dismissal of Nkomo and other Zapu ministers from the government. Two top Zapu leaders, Dumiso Dabengwa and Lookout Masuku, were tried for treason in connection with the caches; they were acquitted but are still detained. This has remained a sore point for Zapu supporters, and started a downward spiral. Hundreds of former Zapu guerrillas returned to the bush and became what Zimbabwe calls 'dissidents'. They attacked farms, road traffic, and trains and have killed at least four hundred people, including many government and Zanu party officials. In July 1982 dissidents kidnapped and apparently killed six foreign tourists in an attempt to force the release of Dabengwa and Masuku. Mugabe sent in the Fifth Brigade, which became notorious for its brutality, including the killings of more than a thousand peasants in Matabeleland. This created thousands of refugees and hundreds more dissidents – some of whom were then recruited, trained, and supplied by South Africa.

But it now seems clear that South Africa had a hand in the original arms caching, and in its exposure. In the first two years after independence, as part of the reconciliation policy, whites who had been part of Rhodesian security, but who stayed on, played prominent roles in the new Zimbabwe security services;

most eventually moved to South Africa, but it is clear that some worked for Pretoria both before and after independence.

The arms-caching trial hinged on the evidence of one witness, who claimed he had cached the arms on the instructions of Dabengwa and Masuku. All other witnesses said that they had been instructed by this key prosecution witness, who only *told* them that Dabengwa and Masuku had authorized the caching. Virtually all the witnesses were still in detention at the time of the trial, in early 1983, more than a year after the disclosure of the arms cache. This key witness, who by his own admission organized the caching, was detained for only thirty-six hours – not even enough time for full questioning in such a complex case. It seems clear that he was a Zimbabwe police agent, and had been at the time of the caching. His contact then was Matt Calloway, a former member of the Rhodesian security services, who was then Zimbabwe's Central Intelligence Organization (CIO) head at nearby Hwange. Calloway moved on to South Africa and was later identified as one of the South African security men recruiting Zapu dissidents and providing arms for them to return to Zimbabwe. Undoubtedly he was working for South Africa in 1980 when his agent organized the arms caching.

The timing of the discovery and nature of the 'investigation' are important as well. Both Zanu and Zapu cached arms in late 1980 and this was well enough known to have been reported in the British press in 1981. The Zapu arms were unearthed in early 1982. Many of Mugabe's security advisers at the time were white, some of whom left for South Africa soon after. They must have known about the caches long before, and may have timed the release of information to Mugabe intentionally at a time when Zimbabwe seemed to have withstood other forms of destabilization and when relations between Zanu and Zapu seemed to be mending.

Finally, one of the key officers who organized the investigation also defected to South Africa. And it was clear that their 'investigation' was aimed at Zapu leaders. One witness at the trial recounted how a white officer told him that 'if the case was successfully completed I would stay well' and get the same protection as the chief witness. 'When I refused to implicate

Dumiso [Dabengwa] and the others he told me I was going to rot in Chikarubi Prison – and I have been rotting in Chikarubi.'

Thus it seems clear that South Africa exacerbated the Zanu–Zapu split, and may even have fooled Zanu into breaking with Zapu and thus setting the conditions for other South African intervention.

Poison pen

Not all South African interventions in Zimbabwe were so subtle or so dramatic. In 1983 and 1984 there was a massive disinformation campaign, involving hundreds of letters and anti-government leaflets. They were posted from a variety of countries to people in Zimbabwe, mostly white businessmen and politicians, and to foreign businesses and embassies. Some were threats, for example against foreign tourists and to the staff of the Australian airline Qantas which had just transferred its flights from Johannesburg to Harare. This was just a few months after six foreign tourists had been kidnapped by dissidents, so threats signed by 'Joe Moyo for the Zipra High Command' caused some consternation. Careful detective work showed that all the leaflets, letters, and envelopes had been typed on typewriters in the South African trade mission in Harare.

Land and aid

Not all of South Africa's political interventions in the region are secret. Undoubtedly the most public was the proposed land deal with Swaziland. Faced with Swaziland moving out of its orbit and even joining SADCC, in 1981 Pretoria unexpectedly offered to give Swaziland several chunks of South African territory which it had long claimed. In expectation of the deal, Swaziland did shift its political line. In 1982 it signed a secret non-aggression pact and expelled the ANC. South Africa then withdrew the offer, but too late to do any harm to its new links to Swaziland. The proposed land deal had been psychologically important at the time in strengthening those within Swaziland who opposed the drift away from South Africa. By the time it was withdrawn, they were in the ascendancy and South Africa had its security agreement. There was no longer a need to offer such a dramatic and public bribe.

Pretoria has also provided small amounts of traditional foreign aid, particularly to Malawi. Soon after independence in 1964, Life President Hastings Banda built close links with South Africa – Malawi is the only black state with a South African embassy, opened in 1967 – and with Portugal, which then ruled neighbouring Mozambique. His links with South Africa were always particularly strange. Malawi is 500 miles away from South Africa, and they share no border. But Banda has always been unusually conservative and curiously pro-white. For example when his elite Kamazu academy opened in 1981 all teachers were Europeans, because he considered no Africans to be suitably qualified. Furthermore, South Africa did help him financially with two pet projects that other donors would not fund. It provided soft loans of R14 million for the new capital at Lilongwe and R11 million for a new railway to the Mozambican port of Nacala.

South Africa financed the initial design work on the capital, which was done by South African town-planners. (This may also explain why it is such a dreadful place to live, and why residential areas are so carefully segregated by income, with huge greenbelts separating the rich from the poor.) For the next decade, many of the senior staff of the Capital City Development Corporation were South African. And Banda still refers to this South African help, precisely because no one else would provide it. So a small amount of money gave Pretoria tremendous prestige.

For a critical three years, 1969–71, South Africa accounted for about 20 per cent of aid to Malawi – a direct reward for opening diplomatic relations. Then it stopped, only to be resumed again in 1980; just when Malawi joined SADCC. South Africa provided R11 million for a grain silo no other donor would fund.

South Africa has also provided small amounts of help to other neighbouring states, largely in the form of technicians and training, particularly of the police. But this was mostly to Swaziland, Lesotho, and Malawi, and mostly in the late 1960s.

Considering its difficult position in the region, and its periodic attempts to win acceptability, it is surprising that South Africa offered so little aid in the 1970s. Now, it is probably too late for such offers to be acceptable, except perhaps to Malawi and Swaziland.

Chapter Eight
The big stick

South African commandos have raided seven of the neighbouring capitals and tried to assassinate two prime ministers. So far, only Malawi and Tanzania have been exempt from direct South African military attack, and even Malawi has been hit by destabilization.

After South Africa's candidate for prime minister failed to beat Robert Mugabe in the election, Pretoria tried to kill Mugabe. On 18 December 1981, a bomb shattered the Zanu headquarters at 88 Manica Road in central Harare, killing seven people and injuring 124 – mostly Christmas shoppers. The bomb had been planted on the roof over the third-floor conference room where the Zanu central committee was due to meet that afternoon. Fortuitously, the meeting was delayed; had it occurred on schedule, Mugabe and most of the Zanu leadership would have been killed. Shortly afterwards, Mugabe's white head of close security, Geoffrey Price, fled to South Africa. As noted in chapter 7, it was Price who helped to organize Muzorewa's campaign. He had stayed on and been given a high post as part of the policy of reconciliation, and used that position of trust to set up spy rings.

In another South African raid, on 16 August 1981, the arms dump at Inkomo Barracks, near Harare, was blown up. A white engineer and explosives expert, Captain Patrick Gericke, was caught but he was taken by the South Africans on 15 November. The South Africans simply kidnapped the wife and two children of the chief investigating officer, Fred Varkevisser, and forced him to release Gericke. All were flown to South Africa.

There were a host of small incidents in which South Africans attacked power lines, railways, and other installations near the Limpopo River, which serves as the border between South Africa and Zimbabwe. On 18 August 1982 in a shootout in a remote area near the border, three white South African soldiers were actually killed. A number of agents were also trained in South Africa and sent back to Zimbabwe; some had been re-cruited by white police and security officials before they defected to South Africa.

Some whites did support the new government after independ-ence, and many white South Africans and ex-Rhodesians re-serve a special bitterness for them as traitors to their race. They became targets of particular attack. For example, a white police-man, Superintendent Eric Roberts, was shot and killed at his home in Bulawayo in December 1982, apparently by former colleagues upset at his investigations of other whites plotting against the new government.

The most subtle attack on both the military and on whites who stayed was the South African raid on the Thornhill air base on 25 July 1982. Explosives put in thirteen aircraft caused more than £15 million damage. After Price, Gericke, and others, it was probably inevitable that the blame was placed on six white airmen, including Air Vice-Marshal Hugh Slatter. In fact, most of the group loved flying and the last thing they would have done was blow up their own planes. They were committed to the air force, if not to Zimbabwe *per se*. The saboteurs were probably former Rhodesian airmen who had gone to South Africa, but who knew their way around the air base. The six were eventually acquitted after the trial judge ruled that their 'confessions' had been obtained through torture and intimidation. They were expelled from Zimbabwe, and virtually all the whites in the air force left with them. The irony is that this was one place where reconciliation had worked; whites were training blacks and were building up a highly effective air force. But training takes a long time, and in 1982 the air force was still mainly white.

South Africa's real coup was not blowing up planes which could be easily replaced, but in tricking Zimbabwe to drive away the personnel. Thus South Africa used the treachery of other whites to lead the new Zimbabwe government to attack its white friends – and thus effectively destroy its own air force.

Commandos

South Africa has special units for attacking the neighbouring states, composed of a mix of South Africans and foreign mercenaries. One set is the four groups of Reconnaissance Commandos, also known as 'Recce Commandos', who are specially trained for sabotage operations. Captain Wynand Petrus Johannes du Toit was caught by Angolan soldiers on 21 May 1985 at an oil installation in Cabinda, 1,700 miles from South Africa and even 800 miles from South African-occupied Namibia.

In a press conference he said he was a member of Fourth Recce Commando, based at Saldanha Bay in the western Cape. He and his team were taken up the coast by an Israeli-built patrol boat, and put ashore in inflatable boats. The plan was to move to an oil storage area and place explosives on several tanks and on the fire-extinguisher system. When the mines went off, they would set the entire tank farm ablaze. The team also carried Unita leaflets and a tin of paint to daub 'Viva Unita' on the road. 'We wanted to leave the impression that Unita did the operation,' Du Toit explained. In the event, Du Toit was caught and two of his colleagues killed before they entered the tank farm.

It was not the first time he had been in Angola. Du Toit's first operation in the Recce Commandos was on 7 November 1982, when he went up the coast to the port of Namibe and then up the Giraul River. There his group destroyed two bridges carrying a main railway and a road across the river.

The bearded young commando also worked with a team in Mozambique. On 17 October 1983, they took a mother ship up the coast, and smaller speedboats to go into Maputo bay. Then they went into the capital itself and bombed the ANC office, injuring five people. It was a successful raid, in that the office was not far from a military barracks and Du Toit and his team sneaked back to the bay and out on their speedboats without being caught. Nevertheless, it was a soft target. The office had no military or guerrilla significance and was no secret; it was on the top floor of an ordinary block of flats, and was where visiting journalists (including some from South Africa) went if they wanted to interview the ANC.

Du Toit's exploits are very similar to two other raids in Mozambique, in which he did not take part but which seem to have had identical plans. On 29 October 1981, road and railway bridges over the Pungue River near the port of Beira were sabotaged in exactly the same way as the Giraul bridges, probably by commandos coming up the river in boats from the coast. And the 9 December 1982 raid on the Beira tank farm, described in chapter 1, was done exactly the way Du Toit planned to hit the Cabinda tanks, with pairs of shoulder-high limpet mines on each tank.

Just as two of Du Toit's colleagues were killed in Cabinda, so other commandos have been killed elsewhere. Two weeks before the successful Pungue bridges raid, and a few miles up the line, a Mozambican patrol came upon a white commando planting a mine on the railway. It shot at his mine, which exploded, blowing him to smithereens. The only proof that he was white was his ear, picked out of a nearby tree. 'Lying propaganda', replied South Africa. The man's pack contained no identification, but there were notebooks with a partly written novel – about Northern Ireland. Careful detective work by the *Observer* showed that the handwriting was that of Ulster-born Alan Gingles. While still in sixth form, Gingles had joined the Ulster Defence Regiment; then he was trained at Sandhurst. Later he became bored and resigned his British commission to fight for the Rhodesian Selous Scouts and then South Africa. At the time of his death, and long before the *Observer* exposé, the SADF issued a communiqué saying Gingles had been based in Phalaborwa (headquarters of the Fifth Recce Commando and the training base for the MNR) and was killed 'in action against terrorists'. At that time about 300 former British servicemen were serving with the SADF, all effectively with British government permission.

Hitting the ANC

As well as hitting bridges and oil installations (many more than I have space to list here), South African commandos also support opposition groups (see the next chapter) and carry out kidnappings and assassinations. Inevitably, the ANC is the main target, but it is almost always the political representatives of the ANC – who are publicly known and easy to find. Joe Gqabi, the ANC representative, was shot and killed outside his house in Harare on 30 July 1981. In Swaziland, the acting ANC representative and his wife were killed by a car bomb on 4 June 1982, and in December 1983 white South African commandos raided a flat in Manzini and machine-gunned an ANC man and a visiting Swazi. In Mozambique, there was the raid on the ANC office and on an ANC house soon afterwards; Ruth First, a prominent member of the ANC and the research director at the Centre of African Studies in Maputo, was killed by a letter bomb on 17 August 1982. In Zambia, a bomb was thrown into the ANC compound in Lusaka on 2 July 1985. None of these were officially claimed by South Africa.

South Africa has also made four highly publicized raids into neighbouring capitals. The story of the 9 December 1982 raid on Maseru opened this book. Similar raids were made on Maputo on 30 January 1981, killing fourteen, and on Gaborone on 14 June 1985, killing twelve people.

In many ways most spectacular, however, was the 23 May 1983 South African Air Force raid on Maputo. It seemed like target practice – a clear demonstration of South African air power. Planes swooped in over a road bridge, then veered off and neatly took out a single grass hut in the middle of a group next to the bridge approach. Another target was a single-storey house in a well-to-do suburb. When I arrived, nothing seemed amiss. Then I went into the garden to find a scene of devastation. Planes had come in at treetop level from the back of the house, splintering the pine trees and blasting off the back wall of the house – there were bullet holes in the inside of the front wall, yet the roof remained intact and the house seemed totally normal from the front.

The South Africans claimed they hit six ANC command

posts and killed dozens of guerrillas. Immediately after the attack, I was free to drive around the entire zone, and I found six targets – which I only later discovered corresponded with a map published after the raid by the South Africans. None was ANC-linked. One was the Somopal jam factory, where three workers were killed. General Malan showed on South African television a model which was clearly of the house described above, said to be the ANC's main planning centre. In fact, it was occupied by the head of the state advertising agency, who had lived in it since he built it himself before independence.

The raid was in retaliation for an ANC car bomb which killed seventeen people outside the offices of Air Force Intelligence in Pretoria three days before. And the raid was particularly nasty. It was called Operation *Skerwe*, which is Afrikaans for shrapnel, and the planes strafed the two suburban neighbourhoods with special fragmentation rockets. Most of the six dead and forty injured were hit by shards of shrapnel, which were embedded in buildings, trees, and gardens wherever the planes had hit. The raid may have been intended to induce panic and fear, not to directly attack the ANC. Several of the six targets were, in fact, near the houses of South African refugees – had South Africa intentionally bombed neighbouring houses as a message to Maputo residents that if they allowed South Africans to stay near them, they were at risk? Or was it simply a hasty and botched retaliation?

The idea of retaliatory raids was adopted from South Africa's Israeli advisers, who have strongly influenced South African military policy (see also chapter 5). The Maputo raid was followed by another Israeli gift. A week later, anti-aircraft fire brought down an Israeli-built remote-controlled spy plane, which was taking TV pictures of Maputo.

The Angola invasion

South African involvement in Angola is on a different scale to its raids on other states: parts of southern Angola have been occupied by South African troops more or less continuously since 1980. After its ignominious defeat in 1976, South African troops were involved in Angola only in low-level support of Unita until P. W. Botha consolidated power and could try again. The declaration of war was the 26 September 1979 air force raid which virtually flattened Lubango, a provincial capital 150 miles north of the Namibia border; the largest furniture factory in Angola was destroyed, killing twenty-six workers. Over the next year, further raids sabotaged railway lines and destroyed several villages. Then in June 1980 South Africa announced Operation Smokeshell, its first full-scale invasion of Angola since the 1976 withdrawal; large numbers of South African troops remained in Angola for five years. The occupation had three main goals – to support Unita, to attack Swapo camps, and to destroy economic infrastructure including roads, railways, and Angola's only iron mine (until the invasion being re-habilitated by an Austrian company that also works for South Africa's parastatal iron and steel company).

More than 130,000 refugees were forced out of the zone, and South African troops began operating the Ruacana/Calueque hydroelectricity scheme, to supply power to Namibia. In February 1984 South Africa agreed to withdraw its troops, and it did move its front line back from 125 miles inside Angola to only twenty miles; finally in mid-1985 the occupying force withdrew, although South African troops continued to operate in Angola to aid Unita, and commandos continued to make raids.

And outside the region

Most South African military action has been in the neighbouring states or inside South Africa itself. But in recent years there have been two well-publicized actions further afield. On 25 November 1981, a South African-organized attempt to overthrow the Seychelles government failed. And on 14 March 1982, South Africa bombed the ANC office in London.

Chapter Nine

Surrogate armies

The bulk of South Africa's war against its neighbours is not being fought by commandos or the air force, but by nationals of the countries themselves. Pretoria now sponsors surrogate armies in four of the neighbouring states – Angola, Mozambique, Lesotho, and Zimbabwe – and each is different.

In Angola, Unita was one of the three original liberation movements fighting for independence against the Portuguese. But in 1971 Unita had agreed to fight the MPLA instead of the Portuguese, hoping to achieve a place in the neo-colonial government they anticipated (see chapter 2). South Africa's 1975 invasion was intended to install Unita in power, and in the late 1970s there were joint Unita–South African operations. But by 1979, the MPLA had effectively defeated Unita.

One of P. W. Botha's first external actions after consolidating power as prime minister was to resurrect Unita. The raids into Angola and the occupation which began in 1979 were largely intended to open up space for Unita. In September 1980 the SADF destroyed and captured Mavinga, a town in south-east Angola. At the time it seemed an odd raid, because Mavinga is 150 miles from the Namibian border and outside the area where the SADF was then active. By mid-1982 it became clear why – Mavinga had been established as Jonas Savimbi's forward base. A more secure headquarters was set up at Jamba on the Namibian border. South African troops occupied a remote triangle in the south-west corner of Zambia, bordering Namibia and Angola, to assure easy military and supply access to Unita zones; in 1982, South African soldiers even captured a ferry boat to prevent Zambian officials from reaching their own territory.

Unita marched north, and when it ran into trouble, South Africa was there to help. In August 1983, Unita tried for the first time to capture a major town, Cangamba, 150 miles north of Mavinga. The invasion failed and Unita withdrew, so the South African Air Force bombed and flattened the town, and Unita moved back to occupy the ruins.

From 1979, supplies were dropped by the planeload, and Unita smuggled out diamonds, ivory, and hardwoods. Backed up with this kind of support, in 1980 Unita was able to cut the Benguela railway from Zambia and by 1982 was disrupting life in large areas of the country. More than 600,000 people were made refugees by the South African occupation and Unita advance; the internal economy was paralysed. In 1985, the Angolan army made major gains against Unita, but the South African Air Force again moved in to protect Mavinga in a series of bombing runs which killed hundreds of Angolan soldiers.

Unita had help from the US CIA in 1975 and 1976, and probably later. Jonas Savimbi has been fêted in Washington and met Chester Crocker, the US assistant-secretary of state for African Affairs. Crocker insisted that Unita must be included in the government.

In July 1985 the US Congress repealed the Clark Amendment, which had prohibited assistance to Unita, and it seemed likely that substantial US aid would be given. At about the same time, the South African defence minister, General Magnus Malan, admitted publicly that South Africa was supporting Unita, and would continue to do so.

Mozambique

The Mozambique National Resistance (MNR or Renamo) has a very different history. At independence, Frelimo was the only liberation movement and it took power unopposed. The Rhodesians wanted a fifth column inside Mozambique, and set up the MNR entirely from scratch – initially based on Portuguese commandos and Mozambicans who had been members of particularly brutal units who were afraid to go home. To augment their numbers, they raided open prisons, where they collected more recruits. Some were former Frelimo officials cashiered for corruption, including Alfonso Dhlakama and André Matzangaissa, the current and former MNR heads. MNR did gain some ground in central Mozambique before it came under heavy Mozambican pressure in 1979; in November the Mozambican army killed Matzangaissa. With the Lancaster House agreement ending the war in Zimbabwe, Rhodesian security stopped supporting the MNR and it almost completely collapsed.

The remaining MNR men fled to South Africa, where the group was put together again. In late 1980 it began attacks. South Africa exercised a high degree of control, selecting the main targets and areas of action. The MNR radio system was set up to limit communications between MNR groups and force them to deal with controllers in South Africa. There were drops of supplies every few days, either from planes or by boat. Advisers and doctors were regularly flown into Mozambique. On 14 October 1984, Dhlakama had a motor scooter accident, and a doctor flew in that night from South Africa to treat him, according to a diary found by Mozambican authorities when they captured the main MNR base at Gorongosa the following year.

The same diary contained orders for MNR officers accompanying a team of South African instructors in Zambezia province, 500 miles away from South Africa, in February 1984: 'In the event of our friends being seen by the people, it will be the fighters' duty to inform the people that they are captured Russians ... Our friends must always speak English and not Afrikaans, to avoid the soldiers finding out, as we have many fighters who were formerly workers in South Africa.'

South Africa also established rear bases for the MNR in neighbouring countries. MNR guerrillas were taken to South Africa for training, and Mozambicans were recruited in South Africa; a special camp was established and several thousand men were trained. Some young men joined the MNR voluntarily, for the excitement and because of its Robin Hood image. But most were press-ganged, in a way not dissimilar to that used in England several centuries ago. Some were peasants kidnapped from their villages. Others were Mozambicans working in South Africa, usually, but not always, illegally.

Sometimes they were picked up by the police and turned over to the SADF who told them that if they did not join the MNR they would rot in jail. Others were illegal immigrants who were simply offered a well-paid job and only found out later what it really was.

As with Unita in Angola, South African support enabled the MNR to spread its activity to more than half the country, plunging the economy into chaos.

Lesotho

The other two groups are entirely South African creations based on internal dissent, and neither has yet won any popular following. The Lesotho Liberation Army (LLA) was created in 1979 by South Africa as the armed wing of Ntsu Mokhehle's Basutoland Congress Party (BCP), also based in South Africa. Since May 1979 it has made dozens of attacks in Lesotho against bridges, electricity pylons, Maseru hotels and airport buildings, and even the United States cultural centre. But the South African role is clear. In November 1982 the Johannesburg *Star* analysed the LLA incidents of the previous year and found all but two were within three miles of the Caledon River border with South Africa. Several involved shelling from South Africa; others were so close to the border that it was obvious someone had driven over the shallow river to plant the bomb or fire a few shots and then driven back.

It seems likely that South African commandos were involved in some of the raids. As in Zimbabwe they went after the leadership. On 4 August 1983 in Maseru, a remote-controlled bomb exploded just as Prime Minister Leabua Jonathan's car passed it; he was unhurt. Information Minister Desmond Sixishe told me that the device was much too sophisticated to have been set up by the LLA on its own. There have also been unsuccessful LLA attempts to attack Jonathan's country house. In addition, there was also a nearly successful attempt on the second most important politician in Lesotho, Agriculture Minister Peete Peete. One attempt succeeded – in 1981 Works Minister Jobo Rampeta was assassinated.

Undoubtedly the BCP has widespread support in Lesotho, perhaps more than the government which robbed it of its 1970 electoral victory. Nevertheless, the role of South Africa was clear to most people in Lesotho, who hated Pretoria more than Jonathan and backed the government's efforts to respond to the LLA.

Zimbabwe

Dissident activity in Matabeleland in the south-west of Zimbabwe increased as former Zapu guerrillas left the army in protest at the continued detention of Dabengwa and Masuku, the dismissal of Nkomo, and the confiscation of the Zapu co-operative society into which many had put part of their demob money. From 1982 to 1984 more than 400 people were killed by dissidents – and several times that many by the army in its crackdown on dissidents. Young men seemed a particular target on the grounds that they must be helping the dissidents, and many fled to neighbouring Botswana. Secretly, South Africa tried to recruit from those refugees. In general, however, the dissidents and refugees would have nothing to do with South Africa. So men who drifted illegally over the border into South Africa looking for work were recruited, just as similar Mozambicans were drawn into the MNR. (The example of Benson Dube was cited in chapter 1.) Arms were supplied and groups of men went across into Zimbabwe to carry out raids. Attempts were made to link up with genuine dissidents, but this usually failed; in one case in September 1983, a South African agent, Hillary Tafara, was actually beaten up by genuine dissidents when they discovered his links. Thus there really seem to be three independent groups active in Matabeleland: genuine dissidents, who seem to have some local support; bandit gangs using the cover of dissidents; and South African-infiltrated groups composed largely of former members of the Rhodesian security forces and men who came from Matabeleland but who are too young to have fought for Zapu in the liberation war.

There is, however, one connection. South African-supplied

ammunition has been used by genuine dissidents, who had been running short of supplies. The dissidents had been using arms, particularly AK47 machine guns, secretly taken from equipment returned at independence. But the Zimbabwe army began to find AK47 cartridges stamped with the number '22–80'. The 22 means they were made in Romania, and the 80 gives the year of manufacture – well after Zapu had received its last supply of weapons, and thus not from caches. Both genuine dissidents and South African groups used the 22–80 shells; the source of supply was clear, because 22–80 shells were found on men captured just after coming over the border, and in caches of South African-supplied arms.

Means and ends

On the simplest but also the most important level, South Africa builds and supports its surrogate armies purely to disrupt. This is intended to demonstrate that majority rule means chaos, and thus underpin its claims for continued white rule in South Africa. It is also an attempt to create so much trouble in the neighbouring states that their governments will not have the time or energy to worry about apartheid. Thus Pretoria is happy to supply bullets to Zimbabwe dissidents even if they hate South Africa.

Besides simply creating confusion, a key goal with all four surrogate armies is to disrupt the economy of the victim. Thus particular targets in all four states are road traffic, electricity lines, shops, farms, and development projects. SADCC is also a major target, particularly railway lines in Mozambique and Angola.

In both Mozambique and Angola, at least some in the military see the possibility of the MNR and Unita having a role in government, and possibly even overthrowing the present government. In the case of Mozambique, this seems not a widely held view.

These groups are sometimes used for particular ends. For example, in mid-1982 when South Africa was increasingly concerned that Malawi was turning away and it wanted to put pressure on President Banda, the MNR was instructed to attack the railway between Beira and Malawi which had previously been exempt.

Finally, South Africa does use the surrogate armies against the liberation groups that it faces. Unita has attacked Swapo and it seems likely that one purpose of the long occupation of southern Angola was to install Unita and create a buffer against Swapo. In Lesotho, the LLA has attacked South African refugees. In Zimbabwe, Zapu has traditional links with the ANC; before Zimbabwe independence some ANC infiltrated into South Africa through Zapu-controlled parts of Matabeleland, and a few ANC went with Zapu guerrillas into assembly points shortly after independence. (This is one reason why Zapu dissidents are so reluctant to accept South African support.) The new South African force in Zimbabwe is most active near the South African border, rather than in traditional Zapu strongholds of Matabeleland. This seems both due to lack of support, and because South Africa wants to use its force to block ANC infiltration.

Although all four surrogate armies are different, there are a number of links. They all come under General P. W. van der Westhuizen, head of military intelligence, who in 1985 became secretary of the ruling State Security Council. The four do share some training facilities in South Africa and their fighters are used somewhat interchangeably. Thus in 1984 the MNR head Alfonso Dhlakama complained that he had lost some of his best men: two had been killed and three captured in Angola, another thirty were fighting in Namibia, and ten were to be taken by the Recce Commandos.

One man who demonstrated the overlap between the surrogate armies was a former Maputo school teacher, Amaro Silva. In 1978 he went to South Africa, where the police sent him to Rhodesia for incorporation in the MNR. After a stint with the MNR he was sent in 1979 to assassinate Robert Mugabe in Maputo; Mugabe was too well protected so he put his bomb in a busy café instead. Then in February 1981, he was part of an MNR group in Swaziland used by South Africa to kidnap an ANC member, Joe Pillay. Next he fought in Namibia. Finally he returned to the ranks of the MNR, where he was caught, tried, and executed.

Chapter Ten

Economic disruption

Businessmen, often acting with South African state support, can sabotage the neighbouring states as effectively as commandos. Because of massive South African government subsidies, several companies have moved from Botswana, Lesotho, and Swaziland to the bantustans, taking hundreds of jobs.

One of Swaziland's largest companies, fertilizer maker Swaziland Chemical Industries (SCI), was put out of business by a combination of monopoly, government, and railway pressure. Although owned by a South African firm, SCI competed with the two big fertilizer companies, undercutting their inflated prices. So they responded by price-cutting in Swaziland, getting South African Railways to refuse to carry SCI fertilizer, and convincing the government to make several changes to import quotas and duties; together, these eventually forced SCI to close.

A similar but more subtle trick seems likely to cause the closure of Lancashire Steel in Zimbabwe. Zisco (Zimbabwe Iron and Steel Corporation) has the only integrated iron and steel production capacity in the region, other than South Africa. Lancashire turned Zisco steel into rod and wire, much of which was exported to South Africa, where it competed with products produced by the Anglo-owned Haggie Rand. In a complex and extended campaign, the South Africans falsely convinced the Zimbabwe government that the Lancashire management was undercharging for rod. The allegation was totally untrue, but so many white businessmen in Zimbabwe were undercharging and asking the buyer to pay the extra into a foreign bank account that the government was quite willing to believe it of

Lancashire. So Zimbabwe nationalized Lancashire and signed an exclusive contract to sell rod and wire to Haggie. The old management in fact had a good contract, which involved the South African buyer paying all transport and customs charges. Haggie tricked the government by offering a higher base price, which allowed the government to say it had been right about Lancashire, but the fine print said Lancashire had to pay the extras – including customs duty. Then Haggie turned around and convinced the South African government to impose a 50 per cent duty on imported wire and rod, making the whole deal uneconomic for Lancashire.

Not all sabotage involves closures. In some cases, South African parent companies have prevented their subsidiaries in neighbouring states from expanding, especially to produce goods which can be imported from South Africa. In other cases South African-controlled companies insist on importing from South Africa instead of buying locally or importing from other SADCC states. Although some South African companies like Anglo are open about their ownership, others have hidden it by registering dummy companies in Europe to own their subsidiaries in neighbouring states. (To be fair, this may also be useful to the parents, allowing them to keep profits out of South Africa's collapsing economy and newly imposed exchange controls, and thus making it easier for them to expand non-African investments.)

Sometimes business and government work together in secret. For example, South Africa imposed unofficial and unpublicized trade sanctions against Mozambique in 1980. South African Railways traffic through Maputo port fell from 4 million tonnes in 1979 to under 1 million tonnes in 1984; some shippers switched voluntarily, but others found they were not assigned wagons unless they agreed to use the more expensive port of Richards Bay. Anglo American unexpectedly and without warning abandoned its two companies in Mozambique that process cashew nuts, that country's most important export. Suppliers sabotaged goods for Mozambique as well. When a cholera outbreak in Maputo was announced in the press, deliveries of chlorine needed to treat the city water supply were suddenly delayed from South Africa. In another case, an aeroplane engine sent to South Africa for servicing came back with a vital nut not screwed on, nearly causing a crash. Yet another time, a key water pump for the Maputo city system was sent to South Africa for servicing, and was not bolted down properly when it was sent back so it was damaged in transit. None of these can be directly attributed to the sanctions against Mozambique, but taken together a picture emerges of unusual incompetence in South African industry or action against Mozambique. In either case, Mozambique was wise to try to cut its dependence on South Africa for vital imports and services.

One of the more complex uses of South African economic power involved electricity. The region is rich in hydroelectricity generating sources, and during the UDI period Rhodesia imported substantial electricity generated by dams in Zambia (despite sanctions). After UDI, when the two were no longer at war, Zimbabwe decided to end the imports by building a coal-fired power station adjoining the Anglo-controlled Wankie Colliery. It would have been cheaper to buy from Zambia or from Mozambique, which was also anxious to sell hydro-electricity. But South African businessmen convinced the Zimbabwe government that self-sufficiency was more important than regional cooperation, thus providing more profits for Anglo while sabotaging SADCC energy cooperation.

The transport battleground

Both South Africa and SADCC agree that transport is the single most important area of economic conflict. The former head of South African Railways, Dr Jacobus Loubser, coined the term 'transport diplomacy'. In his list of economic levers, Geldenhuys put ports and railways first. And in a 1985 study of possible South African retaliation against its neighbours if the west imposed sanctions, the head of the Africa Institute in Pretoria, G. M. E. Leistner, wrote that 'transport is the sector where the neighbouring countries' dependence on South Africa is most critical'.

Yet it is also where South Africa's hold is weakest. There is

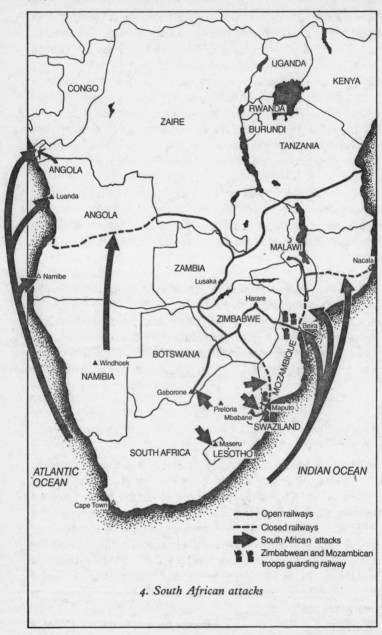

CONGO

UGANDA

KENYA

ZAIRE

RWANDA

BURUNDI

TANZANIA

ANGOLA

▲ Luanda

ANGOLA

MALAWI

Nacala

△ Namibe

ZAMBIA

Lusaka

Harare

Beira

ZIMBABWE

MOZAMBIQUE

BOTSWANA

▲ Windhoek

NAMIBIA

Gaborone

Pretoria

Maputo

Mbabane

SWAZILAND

▲ Maseru

SOUTH AFRICA

LESOTHO

ATLANTIC
OCEAN

INDIAN OCEAN

Cape Town △

Open railways

Closed railways

South African attacks

Zimbabwean and Mozambican
troops guarding railway

4. South African attacks

no economic reason for the SADCC states (except Lesotho and perhaps Botswana) to use South African ports and railways. South Africa has power only so long as they continue to do so. And it uses both military and economic tactics to ensure that they do.

When SADCC was founded in April 1980, all seven SADCC rail links were functioning. The Benguela Railway, which links the Zambia copperbelt to the Angolan port of Lobito, had been kept closed from 1975 to 1979 by Unita, but its apparent demise had allowed repairs to be made and trains to run again. The Tazara Railway, linking Zambia to Dar es Salaam port in Tanzania, had been opened in 1975 after a major construction effort by China. Finally the links in Mozambique were reopened with the Zimbabwe border. Mozambique is in many ways the key to SADCC, and its three ports serve much of the interior: Nacala serves Malawi; Beira serves Malawi and Zimbabwe; Maputo serves Swaziland and Zimbabwe (and, indirectly, Zambia and Botswana).

South Africa's first actions were military. With help from Pretoria, Unita closed the Benguela again in late 1980 and the MNR began attacking the Beira–Zimbabwe line. The Benguela has never reopened, but Zimbabwean troops guarding the Beira line have kept it open. But the Maputo–Zimbabwe line runs so close to the South African border that it was easier to attack, and was finally closed in 1983. The Malawi–Beira line was closed in late 1982, and by the end of 1984 the Malawi–Nacala line was also closed. In 1985 the Swaziland–Maputo line also came under attack, although Mozambican troops were able to keep it open.

The direct effect of the military action is clear. Zambia can export most of its copper via Dar es Salaam, but without the Benguela some must go through South Africa. Malawi has lost both its rail links to the sea, so most goods go via lorry to South Africa; inevitably it is cheaper and easier to buy more goods in South Africa rather than import them from outside, and imports from South Africa have risen again. Swaziland is sending more of its exports via Richards Bay rather than have them shot-up on the line to Maputo. Zimbabwe can send some cargo on the Beira line but, without the preferred Maputo route, most now goes via South Africa. For SADCC as a whole, roughly half of imports and exports are now to or through South Africa.

Despite the raids and line closures, however, there remains surplus capacity on all three operating routes. Thus South Africa also uses its monopoly economic power to ensure that cargo still flows south. One of the South African monopoly groups, Old Mutual, virtually controls international trade in the region. It owns the South African national shipping line, Safmarine, which in turn dominates the shipping cartels which serve South Africa. Those cartels treat the Mozambican ports of Beira and Maputo as 'part' of South Africa, but they charge extra – up to 20 per cent more – for cargo sent through Mozambican ports instead of South Africa. Nevertheless, it should still be cheaper to ship via Mozambique because the rail distance is much shorter. However South African Railways now offers rate-cutting packages with Safmarine, under which Zimbabwean and Malawian shippers receive a reduced rate if they sign high-volume contracts. So for the exporters of tea, tobacco, and cotton it is almost as cheap to ship via South Africa as Mozambique. The *coup de grâce* is that one freight-forwarding agency dominates the entire region, including the Mozambican ports; named Renfreight, it too is owned by Old Mutual. Renfreight uses a variety of tactics, including exaggerating stories of congestion in Mozambican ports, restricting the availability of shipping containers, and making it very difficult to insure cargo passing through Mozambique, so that shippers feel they have no choice but to use South Africa. The role of the forwarder is particularly important, because it handles all of the organization and paperwork for a shipment, and the advice of the forwarder is usually accepted by the shipper.

There are other shipping lines which serve Beira and Maputo which are not part of the cartels with Safmarine, and which provide a regular service at lower rates. There are also other forwarding agencies, including ones run by two multinationals, Lonrho (of Britain) and Société Générale de Belgique. But Old Mutual controls more than half of all SADCC exports and imports, and more than three quarters for Zimbabwe, Malawi, and the BLS states. It is hardly surprising that when most shippers seem to use South African ports and agencies, and when the alternative railways seem to come under regular attack, only the most nationalistic even consider the other choices.

Smash SADCC

It is not only the shippers and the railways that come under attack, but SADCC itself. South Africa has made clear that it sees SADCC as a threat, and it has done special token raids before three of the annual conferences. The second conference was in Blantyre, Malawi, in November 1981. In the month before the conference, South Africa paid special attention to Beira port, then the main port for Malawi, and the railway from Beira to Zimbabwe. First Alan Gingles was killed trying to mine the line. Then the Recce Commandos succeeded in blowing up a key bridge. Finally, a few days before the conference, the commandos came back and blew up the marker buoys in the harbour itself.

The 9 December 1982 raids were partly aimed at the third SADCC conference, which was in Maseru in January 1983. Not only was the conference city hit, but there was a major raid on a SADCC facility – the Beira oil tank farm. (The conference was already scheduled to consider a proposal to rehabilitate the Beira oil-storage facility.) And the day before the conference, arriving delegates were greeted by the bombing of the Maseru abattoir, then still under construction. This underlined the economic nature of the war. Above all, the attack was pointed at SADCC, as the abattoir was funded by Denmark, and one of the opening speakers at the conference was to be the Danish foreign minister, Uffe Ellemann-Jensen.

The fourth conference was in February 1984 in Lusaka, at a time when South Africa was pretending to be a peacemaker in the region, so there were no directly linked raids. But delegates arriving at the fifth annual conference in January 1985 in Mbabane, Swaziland, were greeted with newspaper headlines announcing an MNR raid on the Swaziland–Maputo railway. Earlier that month, commandos had blown up a bridge on the South African–Maputo railway. Both were important reminders to the delegates that South Africa still had military control over the region's railways.

Chapter Eleven

Building on weakness

'The destabilizer will be guided by the target state's political, economic, and military vulnerability', pointed out Professor Deon Geldenhuys. And South Africa has done just that. This is always a difficult area – a victim never wants to admit playing into the hands of the attacker. It is essential to understand the weaknesses that South Africa has been able to use, but also to place them in context.

In particular, South Africa has been able to build on racialism, tribalism, and xenophobia. Sometimes it does so in quite sophisticated ways, but often it simply makes many different attempts, assuming a few will succeed. White South Africa has not hesitated to build on anti-white sentiment in Zimbabwe, for example to hit Lancashire Steel; nor was it unwilling to build on Zimbabwe nationalism, if this could be used against SADCC, as in the case of the Wankie coal-fired power station. (Both were discussed in chapter 10.)

Consider the issue of surrogate armies. In each of the four states, South Africa has been able to build on unhappiness with the government there. In both Mozambique and Angola, government agriculture policies biased towards big state farms did not benefit the peasants, who in many cases saw no reason to actively oppose the MNR or Unita. In Angola, Unita has a historical position as a liberation movement (even if now irrevocably tarnished) and has ethnic support. In Zimbabwe, government atrocities and attacks on the minority party and minority ethnic group created genuine dissent. In Lesotho, the BCP was unfairly denied its election victory and does still have support.

Now put this in context. Most countries have ethnic, regional, or language minorities who often have legitimate grievances and who protest about their cultures being marginalized and their regions being economically disadvantaged. These include Friesians in the Netherlands, Bretons in France, Welsh in Britain, native Americans in the United States and several other countries, and so on almost endlessly. Consider, then, what would happen if a powerful and wealthy neighbouring state inflamed that dissent, trained and organized guerrillas, provided arms and sabotage teams, set up a radio station, and launched an international propaganda campaign to boost the credibility of the new movement.

For example, suppose a foreign power trained Welsh guerrillas, aeroplanes dropped arms and other supplies into the Welsh mountains, submarines came close to the coast to land instructors and pick up men for training, commandos came ashore and blew up British Rail bridges, and a pirate radio station broadcasting in Welsh called for an uprising. All this and more has been done in Mozambique. This example is, of course, hypothetical; there is no war in Wales. But because Welsh nationalists have more support in Wales than the MNR has in Mozambique, it is perhaps reasonable to ask what would happen if a foreign power were to support them. In this case Britain is rich and powerful and would be able to quell a substantial guerrilla insurgency in the Welsh hills, were one to be organized; by comparison, Mozambique is poor and weak and hasn't much chance against the South African-backed MNR.

Furthermore, Europe does have genuine, indigenous 'dissident' problems which have proved notably intractable. Britain and Spain have failed to suppress organized uprisings in Northern Ireland and the Basque regions of Spain; consider what would happen if substantial international support was given to the IRA or ETA.

It is necessary and important to understand the weaknesses South Africa plays on, but it is equally important to realize how vulnerable our own countries would be to similar action, and to appreciate that dissident movements are not just 'African' or 'tribal' problems.

It is also useful to understand the cost of errors. The relatively wealthy, developed countries make major mistakes: building unnecessary chemical plants, nuclear power stations that never work, and high-rise blocks of flats that are uninhabitable and must be blown up. They have agricultural policies that do produce food, but at a mind-boggling cost which no third world country could pay. And that is the central point – the rich can always afford mistakes and a high rate of inefficiency, while it is the poor who must be careful never to waste a penny. So it is that the political and economic mistakes in southern Africa have been dear indeed, costing much more in real terms than similar mistakes in Europe.

Peasants and the land

Both Mozambique and Angola made policy choices to support big farms and industry in a rush for rapid development. The attempt failed at least in part because of destabilization. In retrospect, 1980 was a year of relative peace in both countries, and it was the time that both needed to provide substantial support to the peasantry. In Angola, in particular, Unita had been largely defeated and former Unita supporters were coming out of the bush and looking for government help. It was essential to ensure that there were goods and basic farm tools in rural shops, and that peasants were integrated into the economy. Both countries missed what proved to be a very narrow window, and paid a high price.

The worst drought of the century combined with these unwise agricultural policies to play into South Africa's hands. During the 1982-4 period, the areas of Mozambique, Zimbabwe, and Angola affected by surrogate armies were also badly hit by the drought. South Africa disrupted the economy and prevented drought relief, but all too often it was the government which took the blame for empty shops and lack of food relief.

What kind of development?

Development strategies seem far from destabilization, yet they, too, play a part. Two central development goals are usually to create jobs and provide mass consumption goods like food, soap, and cloth. For the states in the region, this has a special importance – they must create jobs not only for a growing population, but also for men working in the South African mines. Similarly, a SADCC goal has been to produce locally some of the goods now imported from South Africa. If this is not done, South Africa will retain a strong economic hold.

Lesotho, Botswana, and Zambia have all eschewed rural development in a way that effectively benefited Pretoria. They have all stressed capital intensive development, largely involving the production of exports and luxury goods (like bottled beer), and have paid relatively little attention to small farmers. Thus they have provided fewer jobs and must import more food. Lesotho, for example, has concentrated on the £800 million Highland Water Scheme, which will earn money selling water to South Africa, but will not create jobs. Much smaller schemes to keep the water inside Lesotho would allow the development of irrigated agriculture as well as generating electricity, and provide jobs and food for which Lesotho is now dependent on South Africa.

Collaborators

Lesotho's then planning minister, Evaristus Sekhonyana, apologized for being late for our interview. The South Africans had delayed him at the border, and it was clearly deliberate, he said, because he crossed the border so often they knew him well there. As well as being a minister, Sekhonyana is a prominent businessman who travels regularly to South Africa.

Another minister commented to me that 'any business is highly dependent on South Africa which means South Africa has a grip on business people. I have not been to South Africa in ten years – the last three because South Africa said I couldn't. If I was in business and couldn't go to South Africa, I would have to close up shop.' Does this also affect planning decisions as to whether to support projects that delink from South Africa?

In other cases, the South African link is not as obvious, but is equally strong. When I was in Lusaka in December 1984, articles in the press urged people to boil their water because there was no foreign currency to import water-treatment chemicals. Yet South African wine was on sale in the shops on Cairo Road, Lusaka's main street, and the same newspapers carried an article noting that a special water-treatment unit was being imported from South Africa for the brewery. The reason is that, according to government surveys, in 1974 the top 5 per cent of the population enjoyed 35 per cent of the national income; nine years later, there had been a significant redistribution of income, and the top 5 per cent had 50 per cent of the national income. The rich were richer and had more money for wine, while the poor were poorer and there was less money for water-treatment chemicals. In Zambia, luxury goods come predominantly from South Africa, so the worsening income distribution ties Lusaka more closely to Pretoria. Even where money is invested in production, it is far more often for semi-luxury goods which have a high import content for raw materials –for example synthetic fabrics which require imported materials, rather than cotton fabrics which can use the local manufacture. More often than not, these imports come from South Africa. In 1984, Zambia's ruling UNIP party said that the national goal of exporting 80 per cent of copper through Dar es Salaam was wrong, and that only 60 per cent should go that way; the other 40 per cent should go through South Africa in order to have enough wagons to bring back the increasing volume of imports.

Zambia may be the most extreme case, but it is not alone. The elites in the neighbouring states, except for Angola and Tanzania, are often dependent on South African goods and South African shopping trips. They are understandably reluctant to forgo them, even when the policy of their government and ruling party is to delink from South Africa. Inevitably, then, there are excuses and ruses to permit continued trading. The South Africans know this, and use small bribes like free trips and stereos to keep the officials coming to Johannesburg.

Provocation and over-reaction

Finally, South Africa presses on weak spots in ways which sometimes cause its neighbours to commit acts which hurt themselves and thus help South Africa. This is not much discussed within the countries for they are, as intended, politically embarrassing.

This can be seen most clearly in the Thornhill air-base raid in Zimbabwe, described in chapter 8. The worst damage was caused not by South African sabotage of the planes, but by Zimbabwean brutalization of the white pilots they falsely thought carried out the raid. Planes can be easily replaced, but not pilots, so it was the over-reaction rather than the initial raid that really destroyed the air force.

There is no way of knowing if South Africa planned or hoped for this over-reaction, but clearly it benefited from it. What seems most likely is that South Africa pushes in as many places as possible, hoping that in a few cases people will crack under the strain. It knows that the poor countries of the region simply do not have the resources to adequately train (or sometimes even feed and clothe) the police and army, as well as government bureaucrats. Inevitably, these people are overstretched and some break under pressure.

The problem is worst in the fight against the surrogate armies in Angola, Mozambique, Lesotho and Zimbabwe. In Mozambique, a hard-pressed, under-fed, ill-trained national army faces the South African-backed MNR; in some cases, the South Africans have provided the MNR with better equipment than that of Mozambican soldiers. In a few instances the Mozambican army has beaten and killed peasants; in some places it has forced peasants into 'protected villages', as when the Portuguese created 'protected villages' to keep the peasants away from Frelimo. Inevitably this creates bitterness and fertile recruiting grounds for the MNR. In Angola, too, some army actions benefited Unita. And in Matabeleland, the Fifth Brigade atrocities did more to create dissidents than anything South Africa did directly.

The neighbouring states are becoming more conscious of provocation as a South African tactic, and of the consequences of over-reaction. One example is Lesotho. When South Africa first sent LLA men into Lesotho, the police responded by brutalizing villagers known to support the exiled opposition party, but when it became apparent that this did not win support for the government, it switched to a softer line. Government ministers held meetings in border and opposition areas, stressing the obvious South African link. It worked, and villagers now report LLA incursions, even in areas which still support the opposition. This has been combined with better military training, which has meant that the tiny army is able to respond quickly and efficiently, and win some notable victories over the LLA.

Chapter Twelve

Orchestrating destabilization

Previous chapters have looked at various destabilization tactics. In this chapter I will give a few examples of how South Africa pulls these tactics together.

Geldenhuys suggested manipulating food supplies 'to cause serious hardship to the population'. This was done in Mozambique in 1983, at the height of the region's worst drought of the century. At that time, the MNR dominated the more remote parts of Inhambane and Gaza provinces in southern Mozambique. When they moved into the zone in 1982, MNR men burned crops in the field, sacked peasant grain stores, and destroyed shops. During the 1982–3 summer (November to February) the rains failed completely, so there was only a tiny crop in that zone. By mid-1983, there was starvation. People caught by the MNR trying to flee to relief centres in government-controlled areas were killed. Roads were mined and relief lorries attacked to prevent food supplies entering the area. South Africa exerted close control over the MNR, and there can be no question that this was what Pretoria intended. Indeed, at the height of the famine, in August 1983, South Africa air-dropped another 10-tonne crate of weapons and mines to the main MNR base at Tome, Inhambane, in the heart of the famine area.

The famine had an international dimension. In January 1983 Mozambique called in diplomats and appealed for food aid, noting that the rains had failed and that without help people would definitely start to die by mid-year. Donors often claim that countries with disasters do not give enough warning, so that food cannot be delivered in time. Mozambique gave ample warning, but the reaction to the appeal was that food-aid pledges *fell*. No one said so explicitly, but it was clear that the war was the central problem – South Africa's objective in the war was to create a famine, and thus to give food was to take sides. Even the United Nations World Food Programme (WFP) was unwilling to give food for Gaza and Inhambane. Food aid was provided for the southernmost part of Mozambique, which was not affected by MNR actions, but there were always bureaucratic reasons for not providing help for Inhambane; for example, the security problem made it difficult to assess the need.

The United States was ultimately the key. The WFP and most governments were unwilling to take Mozambique's side against a South African-induced famine without clearance from the US. Mozambican President Samora Machel toured western Europe in October 1983 and made several pro-western statements. The US was convinced that Machel was 'turning to the west', and thus called for urgent food aid. This was the sign everyone was waiting for; bureaucratic delays at WFP and in several western capitals melted away. Aid that had been requested in January was suddenly put on aeroplanes in November.

It was useful, but too late for many. There are still no firm figures, but most Mozambican government and foreign sources estimate that more than 100,000 people died between July and December 1983 – victims of a famine consciously created by South Africa as part of its destabilization. These people were as much victims of South Africa's war against its neighbours as if they had been shot in battle.

Tightening the screws on Lesotho

Physically surrounded by South Africa, Lesotho is particularly susceptible to pressure from the apartheid state. And yet, over the past fifteen years it has increasingly distanced itself from the Pretoria government. Prime Minister Leabua Jonathan became an outspoken critic of apartheid, and the African National Congress gained increasing freedom of movement within Lesotho.

In part, South Africa's response was political and military. We have already seen how South African commandos raided Maseru (chapter 1); how South Africa organized an anti-government guerrilla force, the Lesotho Liberation Army (chapter 9); and how Pretoria even organized coups and opposition parties (chapter 7).

But South Africa's real power in Lesotho is economic. All Lesotho's fuel and much of its food and consumer goods come from South Africa. Half its wage labour force works in the South African mines. Lesotho's biggest sources of income are remittances from miners and payments from the customs union with South Africa.

Control of the border is Pretoria's strongest economic weapon, because Lesotho has borders with only one country – if South Africa closes the border, Lesotho slowly strangles. And it has increasingly used this weapon, as I discovered myself in early 1985. As I drove across Maseru Bridge towards the main South African border post, I came to a halt at the end of a queue of cars stretching back to the bridge. Eventually reaching the border post, I found that only one passport-control window was open, and the queue of people stretched off the porch and out into the sun. One officer carefully and slowly looked at every page in each passport, eventually stamping it. Next came the car search. Four officers looked through every suitcase and each book and piece of paper. Not surprisingly, it was several hours before I passed through, and by then the queue of cars stretched across the bridge and back into Lesotho.

This was really just minor harassment – one of the regular reminders to Lesotho about who held the upper hand. I was passing through on a Monday morning and many in the queue were people returning to South Africa from a weekend in Lesotho. A white South African behind me said the delay was common, because South Africa was trying to discourage tourists from going to Lesotho.

But it can be more serious. When South Africa really closes the border, as it does sporadically, then shops in Lesotho soon run out of fresh and packaged food, and fuel runs short. Many of those passing the border are migrant miners returning to South Africa; if they cannot pass, they can lose their jobs.

Most commonly, South Africa uses a mix of economic, military, and political pressures on the tiny mountain kingdom. With independence in Zimbabwe and the formation of SADCC, Lesotho's drift away from Pretoria accelerated. So South Africa stepped up its attempts to reverse the tide and to force Lesotho to increase ties – in particular to sign a non-aggression pact and to agree to the £800-million Highland Water Scheme to provide vitally needed water to the industrial area around Johannesburg. South Africa pulled out all the stops, and used all its destabilization techniques. There were LLA attacks and commando raids on Maseru and on Jonathan; to these were added border closures and threats to repatriate miners; customs union revenue was delayed; South Africa refused to transport British military equipment for Lesotho or a helicopter intended to assist drought relief. In the end Lesotho agreed to go ahead with the water project, but consistently refused to sign a non-aggression pact.

Lesotho was punished for stepping out of line, sometimes even by the private sector. In 1975 Anglo American had agreed to open a diamond mine in Lesotho. It was made clear that such a mine would only be marginally profitable, and thus it was a political gesture which recognized that Lesotho had gained little from its links with Pretoria. But in 1982 when relations were cooling rapidly, and just a few months before the commando raid on Maseru, Anglo announced it was closing the mine on economic grounds. At a stroke, Lesotho lost its largest employer and largest export – a harsh reminder to Lesotho not to bite the hand that fed it.

Nevertheless, the increasing pressure failed to break Lesotho. So in 1985 South Africa turned the screw once more with a special Christmas present. On 20 December South African commandos raided Maseru again, killing six ANC members and three Basotho. And on 1 January 1986, Pretoria imposed an indefinite border closure; like the one I was caught in, it involved searches of vehicles rather than a formal closure. But this time only one car per hour was allowed to pass, and no food, fuel, or medicines were allowed through. The government in Pretoria made clear that the border would be reopened only if the ANC was expelled; it soon added the demand that Jonathan be deposed.

The irony of the latter demand was that at least two coup plots were already under way in late 1985, both intending to overthrow the unpopular Chief Jonathan. In the event, the army struck first and took over on 20 January 1986. The coup was greeted with celebrations inside Lesotho; Jonathan's internal policies, such as his abrogation of yet another election in 1985, made him widely disliked and this was not outweighed by a popular foreign policy.

South Africa was pleased to see a major thorn removed from its side, and signalled its approval by allowing some food and fuel through the border. But the blockade continued for five more days; the border only reopened when the first planeload of expelled South African refugees was in the air.

Nevertheless, Pretoria cannot have been pleased with the new government. The army agreed to share power with King Moshoeshoe II, who had been marginalized by Jonathan. The King had taken strong anti-apartheid stands, and two ministers in the new government were well known for their anti-Pretoria views. One, Khalaki Sello, was actually jailed in South Africa in the 1960s for ANC membership. Evaristus Sekhonyana, who as foreign minister had nearly signed a security agreement with South Africa and who is seen as close to Pretoria, was the only minister from the former government included in the new one. But Sekhonyana was given the post of finance minister, not foreign minister, and the army made clear that Lesotho would still refuse to sign a non-aggression pact.

Furthermore, the King stressed that Lesotho remained open to refugees and that none would be returned to South Africa, while the ANC was allowed to retain an official representation in Maseru. The new government also stressed its continued commitment to SADCC.

In his first speech to the nation after the coup, King Moshoeshoe II declared that 'the economic blockade that this country has been subjected to in the past four weeks has exposed the inadequacy of our post-independence economic strategy'. But what can Lesotho do differently? Long before the coup, a number of studies had suggested that Lesotho would be better off outside the customs union with South Africa, and that it could build a more self-sufficient economy. Pretoria has ensured that this does not happen, with border harassment, the LLA, and threats to reduce the number of miners. The key problem is that it would be best if Lesotho could delink step-by-step, first leaving the customs union and then developing new industries and agricultural projects to provide jobs in place of those on the South African mines. But Pretoria will not allow this; if Lesotho cuts one link, South Africa will suddenly cut the rest, and Lesotho will find its border closed, its miners sent home, and its electricity cut off.

South Africa's second attempt at coup-making seems also to have failed – just as it had put Jonathan in power only to have him turn against them, so it helped to depose Jonathan only to face an equally critical new government. In part, this reflects South Africa's underestimation of nationalist feeling in the neighbouring states. It also reflects South Africa's relatively small role in the 20 January coup – perhaps smaller than Pretoria intended. The coup would probably have taken place in January or February even without the blockade, and thus had an internal dynamic of its own.

But Pretoria has flexed its muscles and seems unlikely to pull back. A combined assault of more raids and longer and tighter border closures can be expected as Pretoria presses the new government to drop ministers unacceptable to it, continues to prevent economic delinking, and attempts to force a security accord.

Pulling Swaziland and Malawi back into the fold

The two majority-ruled countries considered to be South Africa's only friends in the region began to slip from its grasp around 1980, when the independence of Zimbabwe opened up new regional possibilities. As noted in chapter 4, both Swaziland and Malawi joined SADCC and made other tentative moves to reduce economic links with the apartheid state.

For both states there was a mix of carrot and sjambok; more carrot for Swaziland and more stick for Malawi. In Swaziland, there were a few raids over the border against the ANC, and on one long weekend in 1984 South Africa closed the border, preventing holidaymakers from going to Swazi hotels and casinos. But it also offered the land deal, the railway line, and gave Swaziland a £30 million gift. This pulled the Swazis back into line. Swaziland became the first neighbour to sign a non-aggression pact on 17 February 1982. In 1984 South Africa established bases in Swaziland for the MNR to attack Mozambique, and in 1985 Swaziland allowed the opening of a South African trade mission – the first new diplomatic mission in black Africa since an embassy was opened in Malawi in 1967.

Malawi, too, was offered some financial aid, although on a smaller scale. When it hosted the SADCC annual conference in November 1981, South Africa showed its displeasure by disrupting oil supplies to Malawi and by the raids on Beira, Malawi's most important port. The next year, the MNR received specific instructions to close the railway from Malawi to Beira. Malawi's position with respect to the MNR has been confused and there were probably divisions within the government on this issue. South Africa set up bases for the MNR for the invasion of northern Mozambique, and for resupply flights. It has cracked down periodically, especially after Mozambican complaints; for example, a captured MNR diary notes the expulsion from Malawi of the MNR representative in May 1984. Yet, each time the South Africans were able to re-establish rear bases. In some cases, it would seem that they provided compensation. For example, South African Railways offered reduced freight rates on goods carried by lorry to and from Malawi. On balance, however, the results of the pressure have been mixed; Malawi's trade with South Africa has returned to its former levels and it provides support for the MNR, yet it remains genuinely active in SADCC.

1981 – squeezing Zimbabwe

In 1981 South Africa launched a major campaign against Zimbabwe. It gave notice that it would end a bilateral trade agreement, which allowed £40 million of manufactured goods into South Africa each year and would have cost Zimbabwe several thousand jobs. Many Zimbabwean migrant workers were expelled from South Africa. It imposed a railway embargo, and withdrew locomotives and maintenance staff it had loaned to the former Rhodesia Railways. Imports, particularly of fuel, were delayed, and exports were disrupted. There were also raids on the railway to Beira, culminating in the sabotage of the bridge in October. In all, the disruption meant that by the end of 1981 Zimbabwe had a backlog of £75 million worth of maize, sugar, asbestos, and coal it was unable to export. In parallel there were military actions, including the raid on Inkomo barracks and in December the attempt to kill Mugabe. Agents were already being infiltrated into Zimbabwe, and the arms caching had been promoted.

The exact goal of the 1981 destabilization campaign was never clear. South Africa's only overt demands were that Zimbabwe negotiate with it on a minister-to-minister basis, thus giving a form of diplomatic recognition, which it refused to do; and that it tone down the anti-apartheid rhetoric, which it did do. Indeed, Zimbabwe in 1981 may show the clearest case of conflicts over policy. The South African military saw Mugabe as a Marxist who had to be destabilized in whatever way possible, and others in the government wanted to break the Zimbabwean economy. It was also highly embarrassing that Zimbabwe was exporting maize in competition with South African maize; not only did South Africa lose money, but there was the important and unacceptable ideological point that a black-ruled socialist state could produce a food surplus.

Others disagreed. South African Railways head Jacobus Loubser was opposed to having his railways used for *de facto* sanctions against Zimbabwe, and many businessmen were anxious to continue trading despite the change in government. In the end, it was the United States which convinced South Africa's State Security Council that it was more useful to keep Zimbabwe economically tied. Under US pressure, at the end of 1981 the railway embargo was ended and the trade agreement renewed.

But the sanctions cost Zimbabwe dear. The delay of £75 million in exports caused a cashflow crisis, and forced Zimbabwe to turn to the IMF for help, which it probably would not have done – at least that early – without pressure from Pretoria.

The hand on the oil tap

Oil is one of the most precious commodities in the region, and South Africa has used both military and economic actions to try to ensure that as many of the neighbouring states as possible remain dependent on it for fuel.

Angola is the region's only oil producer, and petroleum allows it to pay for its defence against South African aggression. Commandos have hit oil facilities at least four times: Lobito oil terminal, 12 August 1980; Luanda oil refinery, 30 November 1981, causing a loss of £20 million and closing the refinery for four months; Cabinda oil pipeline, 12 July 1984; and the failed attempt on the Cabinda oil terminal, 21 May 1985.

In Mozambique, the tanks in Beira were attacked on 9 December 1982, affecting oil for Zimbabwe and Malawi. We have seen that the oil pipeline from Beira to Zimbabwe is regularly attacked by the MNR, and fuel carried by rail through South Africa to Zimbabwe is also disrupted. South Africa caused several fuel shortages in Zimbabwe in the first three years of independence.

The three customs union members buy all their fuel from South Africa, although there is nothing in the customs union regulations which require them to do so. But when Lesotho was given a donation of oil, South African Railways simply refused to transport it. Fuel tanks in Maseru (Lesotho) have been attacked twice; in the second raid a South African helicopter was involved. And when Botswana built additional storage facilities, to give it a small fuel reserve, South Africa refused to fill the tanks for more than a year. Considering the raids on oil facilities in other neighbouring states, and the reluctance to allow Botswana and Lesotho any independent supplies or reserves, it is perhaps not surprising that the three customs union members still buy from Pretoria – despite the extra £15 million per year cost.

Chapter Thirteen

Choosing sides

Ronald Reagan's election as US president in November 1980 gave a significant impetus to South Africa's war against its neighbours. Under Jimmy Carter, US displeasure did serve as a constraint on South African action. South African prime ministers hated Carter bitterly; US pressure was even seen as part of the Marxist total onslaught. But they did hold back. Reagan put all issues into an east–west framework, and saw anti-communism as the key issue instead of human rights. Thus the new administration backed Pretoria as the anti-communist bulwark in the region. Chester Crocker, who as Reagan's under-secretary of state for African affairs set policy for the region, stressed the continued US opposition to apartheid, *per se*. But rather than Carter's pressure and support of at least limited sanctions, the US was to use a policy of 'constructive engagement' to try to convince white South Africa that reforming apartheid was in its own interests.

The Reagan victory came just as P. W. Botha's new military government was consolidating power, and it was seen as a licence for destabilization. The 30 January 1981 commando raid on Maputo came just ten days after Reagan took office. Although South Africa was already militarily involved in other states, this was the most public raid so far, and was a test of opinion in Washington. There are unconfirmed rumours that the US actually agreed in advance; at least it did not object.

In March, a high-ranking South African delegation, led by the head of military intelligence Piet van der Westhuizen, went to Washington for talks. It would seem that he came away with the view that the new administration would not object to destabilization, because South African action was stepped up dramatically in the months that followed. Van der Westhuizen is the man responsible for surrogate armies, and he rapidly expanded support for his groups.

Commando raids and army action also increased in 1981. The largest and most bloody action was Operation Protea, in which more than 10,000 South African soldiers with tanks and armoured cars invaded and occupied parts of southern Angola. Other incidents in 1981 included: another incursion into Mozambique near the capital and the attack on the bridges near Beira, bombs in the capital of Lesotho, attacks on the ANC in Swaziland, the occupation of the south-west corner of Zambia, border clashes with the Botswana Defence Force, the attempted assassination of Robert Mugabe, and the attempt to overthrow the Seychelles government.

Three victories have been claimed for constructive engagement. It is said that under US pressure South Africa ended its 1981 sanctions against Zimbabwe, and that it was also under US pressure that South Africa signed the Nkomati Accord with Mozambique. Third, some US sources claim that the US stopped South Africa from overthrowing President Samora Machel. In fact, it remains unclear if South Africa's State Security Council would have agreed a coup in Mozambique, even without US pressure, because it would have involved intolerable costs to keep a puppet government in office there. But the main point is that without constructive engagement, South Africa would never have felt free to embark on these adventures – so the only victories of constructive engagement seem to be curbing its own excesses.

Aid as politics

The polarization also affected SADCC. Its early organizing efforts had discreet support from the EEC and the Commonwealth, who saw it as a way of drawing Marxist Mozambique and Angola into a pro-western organization – which surely was one of its effects. The Carter administration privately backed EEC efforts, and in a regional swan song gave strong public backing to SADCC at its first conference in Maputo in November 1980 (after Reagan had been elected, but before he took office).

Under Reagan, the US would not accept such subtlety. The US, Britain, and West Germany – respectively South Africa's number one, three, and four trading partners (Japan is number two) – have all given verbal support to SADCC but been disruptive in practice. Britain and the US both say they support SADCC's development goals, but publicly oppose the central goal of delinking from South Africa.

At the January 1984 SADCC conference angry delegates exposed one example of US meddling. The US had offered to fund a vital regional agricultural research project into drought-resistant crops such as sorghum. SADCC has always been open to donors funding projects in particular states, so that it never asked the US to fund projects in Angola (with which it has no diplomatic relations). In this case, the research centre was to be in Zimbabwe. But at the last minute, the US demanded that none of the *benefit* of what was to be a regional project should go to the three socialist states: Angola, Mozambique, and Tanzania. They would not be allowed to send students or receive the seeds developed. This was clearly an attempt to split SADCC, and was rejected.

The World Bank initially opposed SADCC because of US attitudes. At one SADCC donors conference, the World Bank delegate was heard asking the US delegate for instructions as to how to vote. The US, UK, and World Bank have all shifted somewhat recently; while still opposing SADCC's goal of de-linking from South Africa, they nevertheless have begun funding projects that will aid SADCC to delink. The US is still attempting to be divisive, however; it is putting money into projects in Mozambique (in a reversal of its 1984 line) while upping its support for Unita in Angola. The EEC's attitudes are schizophrenic, which is hardly surprising, considering the differing views of both its member states and of the various parties in the member states. Thus a few key officials in the EEC secretariat who deal with southern Africa are openly pro-Pretoria and anti-SADCC, while others support SADCC strongly.

Aid can have subtle effects which are sometimes not clear at the outset. A good example is the EEC- and World Bank-assisted Highland Water Scheme in Lesotho, which is likely to cost more than £800 million in the next ten years. This will provide water to South Africa, which will pay Lesotho an estimated £50 million per year. The obvious argument in favour is that water is one of the few resources Lesotho has, and it should be exploited to earn money. But there are three arguments against. First, South Africa is chronically short of water, so the Lesotho water is essential for electricity generation and the Sasol oil-from-coal plants – in other words, to make it more resistant to sanctions. Second, the project further ties Lesotho's economy to South Africa. Third, the money to be earned is less than one third of what Lesotho earns from migrant miners, yet if that massive investment were made on irrigation, electricity generation, and agricultural and industrial development projects inside Lesotho it would be enough to create jobs for many men now in the mines. So foreign aid that seems to help Lesotho is probably of more use to South Africa.

A similar point can be made about the regional role of the World Bank and IMF. Their standard prescription calls for a more open economy, which means, in practice, that underdeveloped countries are expected to continue to import manufactured goods and export agricultural produce. For SADCC this means a halt to industrialization and the continued import of manufactured goods from South Africa. A World Bank-sponsored study actually suggested the closing down of Zimbabwe's iron and steel plant and much of its engineering industry – facilities that will be key to SADCC development.

Even small decisions by aid agencies can have an important effect. For example, US food aid to Zimbabwe was sent through South African ports; this meant that South African Railways had many empty wagons in Zimbabwe, and so it offered cheap rates to shippers who filled them – thus undercutting SADCC attempts to use Mozambican ports. By contrast, EEC milk powder for Zimbabwe is sent through Beira, and Zimbabwe maize bought by the World Food Programme to be sent to other countres in Africa is exported via Beira; the success of the

WFP 'maize train' to Beira was probably a subsidiary reason for the October 1981 sabotage of the railway bridge near Beira.

Support for the frontline states

Thus it is clear that foreign countries can act in ways which support the frontline states and help their defence against South Africa. The most important is explicitly political assistance, particularly to repair damage done by South Africa. For example, Italy rapidly rebuilt the Luanda refinery, while in a very public act of solidarity, Sweden and the Netherlands rebuilt the road bridge near Beira, destroyed in the October 1981 raid. In chapter 10 I referred to the South African attack on a Danish-funded abattoir in Maseru the day before the January 1983 SADCC conference. The Danish foreign minister, Uffe Ellemann-Jensen, responded by announcing an increase of aid to SADCC from £5 million to £20 million.

Britain's role in the region has been ambivalent, but it has provided important military help to fight the MNR – one of the few western nations to do so. This has been indirect, but no less useful for that. Britain has provided equipment for the Zimbabwean troops fighting in Mozambique against the MNR, and Mozambican officers are to be trained in Zimbabwe by the same team training the Zimbabwean army. (And a few Mozambican officers are being trained at Sandhurst.)

The other essential area of support is general help for SADCC. Development aid builds up the neighbouring states and makes them better able to withstand South Africa's war, so assistance to SADCC is one of the most constructive ways to fight apartheid. Particularly important are help to rebuild transport links, which have become South Africa's number one target, and help to increase trade between the SADCC states to reduce their dependence on South Africa.

Donor agencies, however, must be clearer in their position, and not use South Africa as their base and the source of their aid. Similarly, foreign companies should stop treating the neighbouring states as part of the South African market, and establish regional offices in Harare or Lusaka. Disinvestment is now under way with a vengeance, as western capital votes with its dollars; some of this capital could be redirected into the neighbouring states.

Although some British and US firms have pulled out of South Africa, the west remains divided on the region. Support for SADCC has come largely from those countries which do not have big investments or big markets in South Africa, and are looking for an alternative base in the region. These include Scandinavia, Italy, Canada, the Netherlands, Belgium, and, to a lesser extent, France. They are aware that the SADCC states could provide nearly all the minerals now bought from South Africa, if the mines were developed, and that SADCC will soon be a larger market than South Africa. Britain, West Germany, and the US seem more concerned to protect their existing investments, markets, and sources of minerals.

Chapter Fourteen

Nkomati

By late 1983 there was an increasingly widespread view both inside and outside South Africa that destabilization was getting out of hand. In Angola, the SADF had faced unexpected military resistance to its latest invasion, while South Africa had been given an unprecedented warning by the Soviet Union not to push too hard in Angola. In Mozambique, the 23 May bombing of the jam factory had made the military look extremely foolish. Furthermore, the worsening depression inside South Africa meant that the business community wanted access to Mozambique which was impossible due to security problems. Even academics like Geldenhuys were publicly criticizing the level of destabilization, arguing that the State Security Council had abandoned the balanced approach of the total strategy for a purely military line. And there was a widespread feeling that it had not worked; destabilization had created chaos in the neighbouring states, but it had brought no concrete gains for South Africa.

At the same time, South Africa was coming under diplomatic pressure. Mozambique President Samora Machel's trip to western Europe in October 1983 did turn up the pressure on Pretoria to be seen to negotiate. Informally, Chester Crocker argued that now was the time to change the balance, and that it was in South Africa's interest to trade some of its military advantage for diplomatic and economic leverage. Behind this was a US anxiety that by the time of President Reagan's campaign for re-election in November, the US should be seen to have gained something in southern Africa.

Thus South Africa was under internal and external pressure to ease up on destabilization, at least temporarily. As a result, it signed an agreement in February in Lusaka in which it agreed to pull its troops out of part of southern Angola. And on 16 March 1984, with much fanfare, Machel and P. W. Botha met at the border to sign the Nkomati non-aggression pact. Mozambique conceded three key points to the South Africans. First, it became the first neighbour to publicly sign a non-aggression pact; this had been a demand for some years, and up until then only Swaziland had signed, and it did so secretly. (The Swazi pact was announced two weeks after the Nkomati signing.) Second, the Mozambicans agreed to expel all ANC, military as well as ordinary refugees, except for a ten-person diplomatic mission (whose members were apparently subject to a South African veto). Third, Mozambique agreed to parallel talks on economic issues, including reopening Mozambique to South African tourists. The agreement was a humiliation which brought widespread criticism from other African states, but Frelimo had little choice; destabilization and drought had shattered the economy.

Nevertheless, in exchange Maputo won what it thought was the central point – Pretoria's agreement to end all support for the MNR.

Putting on a show

At first, it seemed Pretoria might abide by the accords. It began to pull back the troops in Angola. In Mozambique, it stopped the MNR radio station and sharply reduced the number of supply flights. Then in June the withdrawal from Angola stopped; the South Africans had pulled back from 125 miles inside Angola to a new front line twenty-five miles north of the border, but they did not withdraw. More than a year later, South Africa finally withdrew the troops in question, but it stepped up its commando raids and support for Unita.

And far from bringing peace, the war in Mozambique escalated after the accord. For the first time the MNR became active near Maputo itself, including attacks on the road, railway, and electricity line between the capital and South Africa. It soon became clear from captured MNR men and other information that in the weeks before Nkomati, South Africa had provided enough supplies for at least six months, and had ordered the MNR to move on Maputo.

This was confirmed when a joint force of the Mozambican and Zimbabwean army captured the main MNR base in Mozambique on 28 August 1985. Known as 'Banana House', it was in the foothills of the Gorongosa mountains, in the centre of Mozambique about a hundred miles north of Beira. In the base were various notebooks and a desk diary which chronicled supply flights, radio messages, and meetings there and in South Africa.

The diary notes that the South Africans told the MNR they were under pressure from the United States to sign Nkomati and to 'ensure negotiations between Machel and Renamo [MNR] before November' – the date of the US elections. In February and early March 1984 there were twenty-five supply drops, from planes and boats, to keep the MNR going for six months. South African instructors flew in to organize the urgent expansion of operations in Zambezia province.

In January and February 1984 the South Africans warned that an accord would be signed, but repeatedly promised to continue their support. Two people named in the diary who met with MNR leaders in South Africa and promised support were the head of military intelligence, General van der West-huizen, who as a member of the State Security Council would have taken part in the meetings that agreed to sign Nkomati, and the then chief of the armed forces, General Constand Viljoen. They instructed the MNR to attack railways 'and other targets of an economic nature, SADCC', and foreign workers 'because they are the most dangerous in the recovery of the economy', according to the diary.

On 16 June 1984 MNR head Alfonso Dhlakama sent an urgent message to the South Africans, noting that 'we no longer have the war material to go on squeezing Machel' – as clear an indication as anyone needs that the MNR is entirely dependent on its South African backers. Dhlakama reminded them of their promise 'of keeping up support to us clandestinely'. The contact man, Colonel Charles van Niekerk, replied four days later that 'the political climate here and internationally is still bad for continuing to supply Renamo' and thus the MNR should 'use as little war material as possible. Avoid combat with the Mozambican army, giving more attention to destroying the economy.'

Exactly a month later, Colonel van Niekerk sent a new message saying that the problems were being resolved. An MNR delegation was taken to South Africa by submarine for meetings in mid-August with Foreign Minister Pik Botha, Defence Minister Magnus Malan, and Van der Westhuizen. In those meetings, and in a meeting on 9 September with Viljoen, it was decided that the assistance should be called 'humanitarian aid', that civilian planes should be used, and that the South Africans should upgrade the airstrip at Banana House to allow those planes to land (rather than continue the practice of parachute drops). The first resupply flight arrived on 21 August 1984, and contained 'building material for a landing strip' as well as twenty-five cases of AK47 ammunition and fifty-three reams of paper. The diary records a steady increase in flights, including at least eight in October.

At the August meetings, the South Africans also agreed to send 'material for urban guerrilla warfare' including 'time bombs and timing devices'. A month later, Van der Westhuizen warned South African businessmen of the dangers of urban terrorism in Maputo.

Conflicts inside

The warning to businessmen shows the divisions which were opening up after Nkomati. The accord had been hailed by the business community because it gave them access to Mozambique. Now they were subject to MNR attack, and several South Africans working for South African firms in Mozambique after Nkomati were kidnapped by the MNR.

The notebooks and diary also show that the MNR's military backers were painting a picture of sharp divisions with the Ministry of Foreign Affairs. One entry says that in the September meeting General Viljoen 'warned us not to be fooled by the schemes of Pik Botha' and not to accept the amnesty being offered by Frelimo. Viljoen noted that 'the world is convinced that Machel is changing, because he doesn't seem to them to be entirely communist'. But this is not true and there should be 'a joint strategy for putting Machel out'.

The notebooks make clear that Pik Botha was coming under increasing pressure at meetings with the US, British, French, and Italian ambassadors and with Crocker (who argued that the MNR had no popular base in Mozambique; in contrast, in his view, to Unita in Angola). With the US election looming, South Africa did arrange three-way talks between Mozambique, South Africa, and the MNR which resulted in the 'Pretoria declaration' of 3 October which simply recognized that there ought to be a cease-fire. The South Africans were able to present themselves as peacemakers, and had satisfied the US condition of face-to-face Mozambique–MNR talks before the elections.

Open violation

After the re-election of Reagan the pressure was off, and there was no attempt to hide continued support for the MNR and Unita. Two other factors also seem important. Businesspeople found that Mozambique had been even more bankrupted by destabilization than they had expected, so there was less money to be made and they had less interest in Mozambique. More important, South Africa's own townships had exploded again. They dominated both the State Security Council and international headlines, so no one was concerned with what the SADF did to Mozambique. And whatever the divisions between the military and the foreign ministry, two examples make clear that their actions were coordinated.

One example was triggered by a natural disaster. The MNR had repeatedly attacked the power line from South Africa that supplies half of Maputo's power. But they never hit more than one or two pylons, which were easily repaired. Then nature took a role: on 26 March 1985 a freak windstorm brought down thirty-one pylons, more than could be repaired quickly. For once, international donors responded promptly; the US government pledged $250,000 to buy coal from South Africa for the coal-fired power station that supplies the other half of Maputo's power. The mines agreed to sell the coal, but South African Railways (SAR) simply refused to carry it. Finally, after a public protest by Mozambique, on 27 April SAR said it would give the coal priority; unfortunately, the previous night commandos sabotaged a railway bridge five miles from the South African border.

The other example, which shows most clearly the open support for the MNR, is the three visits by the South African deputy foreign minister Louis Nel to Banana House, landing on the new airstrip on 8 June, 2 July, and 19 August 1985. On the second visit, according to the Banana House diary, Nel said that in negotiations with Mozambique he would pretend that the MNR had substantial help from abroad – that is, other than South Africa. And he said 'we want to make Frelimo enter into negotiations [with the MNR]. This will make Frelimo lose its diplomatic weight.'

When all this was revealed by Mozambique, Nel admitted the visits, and South Africa continued to fly in supplies. There can be no stronger indication of continued high-level support for a surrogate army than for a deputy foreign minister to illegally enter a foreign country to talk to that army's leader.

Meanwhile, in mid-1984 Malan flew to Unita's bush headquarters at Jamba, just north of the Namibia border, to reassure Jonas Savimbi of Pretoria's continued support. In September 1985, Malan announced that South Africa was still supporting Unita, and would continue to do so because it was in the 'interests of the free world'. In July, the US Congress had repealed the Clark Amendment, thus allowing the US to support Unita as well.

Chapter Fifteen

What can be done?

Constructive engagement has made life worse for the neighbouring states, and is not a solution to the problems of southern Africa. On the other hand, it is clear that even limited pressure on South Africa has some effect. Carter's stand on human rights did serve as a constraint on Pretoria; limited international pressure did force South Africa to sign the Nkomati Accord (although not to abide by it). Pressure must be brought to bear on South Africa, not only to eliminate apartheid (which is essential), but also to end destabilization.

The only international pressures available and widely promoted are sanctions, boycotts, and disinvestment. No one denies they are limited in effect. They will not end apartheid and destabilization; only the internal struggle will do that. But sanctions do have a role to play, both in imposing real and useful limitations on the apartheid military machine, and as an essential psychological and moral support for those inside struggling to end apartheid. Thus sanctions and disinvestment must be seen as the easiest form of external support, and not as *the* means to end apartheid and destabilization.

Sanctions work

Much is made of the limitations of sanctions, boycotts, and disinvestment. Stress is put on how successful South Africa is in breaking and avoiding sanctions, and about how self-sufficient it has become. Although that is true, it hides the real cost of sanctions.

South Africa is rapidly building up its military and industrial capacity. For example, it is one of the few countries in the world to make diesel engines. But it pays a high price. Its diesel engines are expensive and inefficient, and transporters complain bitterly about them. They are a key element in military and civilian transport that cannot be cut off, but all road transport is more expensive than it would be if South Africa was not worried about sanctions.

Similarly, since the mandatory arms embargo was imposed in 1977, South Africa has developed the capacity to build many of its own weapons systems – with Israeli help and sanctions busting in a number of countries. Nevertheless, it is still dependent on imports for 25 per cent of its weaponry. The air force is particularly dependent on imported components for maintenance and modernization.

Simon Jenkins, political editor of the *Economist* and an opponent of sanctions, had to admit (in the *Economist*, 30 March 1985) that 'by denying South Africa a full modernization of its air force', the arms embargo did clearly restrict its ability to challenge the 1983 warning by the Soviet Union not to go too far in Angola. Thus 'it forestalled what might have been an incipient arms race'. In other words, it was the arms embargo and superior Angolan weaponry as much as any diplomatic pressure that forced South Africa to pull back in Angola.

Similarly, the oil embargo seems honoured only in the breach. Yet the Shipping Research Bureau in Amsterdam estimates that sanctions have imposed an extra cost of £1,000 million a year on the South African economy, made up of the extra cost of producing oil from coal (a very expensive process), maintaining a sizeable reserve, and paying fees to sanctions-busting middlemen. South Africa is still obtaining its oil, but its depressed economy is paying a heavy price.

There was much debate about the effectiveness of disinvestment and withholding loans. But when the banks began calling in loans, and companies pulled out money, the rand collapsed. In part the banks were acting out of ordinary capitalist considerations – unrest and a weakening economy put their loans at risk. But the sanctions campaign played an essential role, because the banks were also afraid that if they continued their loans they would be attacked for collaborating with apartheid. The result was that South Africa defaulted on its debts, and the internal economic crisis was made so much worse that corporate leaders began talking to the ANC.

The psychological impact of sanctions should never be underestimated. White South Africa sees itself as an outpost of Europe in a hostile black land, and it is hurt most by sanctions which cut that link. The sports and cultural boycotts, and bans on South African Airways landing rights, are good examples. South Africa is sports mad, and the 1977 Gleneagles agreement and the Olympic boycott do more than anything else to remind whites of the price of apartheid. I am constantly struck by the way the South African press gives continuous front-page coverage to the most obscure team which breaks the sports boycott.

Limitations

The limitations of sanctions are really those imposed by the west, not the response of South Africa. If the existing oil and military sanctions were made watertight, the war would be over relatively soon.

Loopholes are the first problem to consider with any package of sanctions, boycotts, and disinvestment. For example, the South African monopoly groups do make use of disinvestment; despite the depression they have substantial surplus cash and are anxious to buy out foreign investors. But they do need the technology. Thus what South Africa really wants is fake disinvestment, where foreign investors sell a majority holding to local shareholders. This allows the foreign partner to claim it has no control over the South African company, but ensures that it still supplies essential new technology. Japan bans investment in South Africa, but allows licences and technology transfer, so Japan is now South Africa's second largest trading partner and Japanese firms have 40 per cent of the South African car market.

Similarly, the arms embargo is so loosely enforced that smugglers have found that one of the easiest routes for taking officially banned military technology from the US to the USSR is to export it first to South Africa.

Choosing weapons

A decade ago, sanctions had an effect against Rhodesia, and probably did bring the war to a close more quickly. They were less effective than they might have been largely because of US, British, Portuguese, and South African connivance with sanctions busting, especially of fuel. Similarly, South Africa is already paying a high price for sanctions and disinvestment – a price that would be much higher if even the present limited sanctions were followed by more countries.

Sanctions, boycotts, and disinvestment are the most effective weapons against apartheid that are available to people outside South Africa. But because of the problems already noted, it is important to pick those that will be most useful and which can be enforced.

For example, computers and electronics are particularly important to try to control, as South Africa has developed no expertise in these areas. And it should be possible to monitor at least some of the transfer of technology in these areas.

The most useful sanctions are precisely those which hit the economy hardest. The biggest non-productive expenditures are paying for the bureaucracy to run apartheid, and funding the war against the neighbours and against the people of South Africa. If the economy is weaker, there is less money for the war.

Highly public actions have a useful pyschological effect. Bans on krugerrand and fruit sales are useful both because of the cost, and because of the psychological impact, although their overall effect is limited.

In the longer term, enforcement and publicity are probably the key issues. It is necessary to track down those who are breaking the oil embargo, and to highlight disinvestments that still allow technology transfer.

Reluctance

The US and Britain have shown particular reluctance to impose sanctions. They cite a variety of other reasons, but their real concern is for their trade and investments in South Africa.

Both countries accept the principle of sanctions, and that there should not be a *totally* free market. They agree, for example, that certain kinds of high technology, nuclear material, and weapons should not be sold to certain states. The US has imposed wide-ranging sanctions on Poland and other states, and Britain has done the same to Argentina. These sanctions have hurt US and British industry, and no doubt cost jobs, but there was a view (shared by at least part of the business community) that sometimes moral and political considerations override profit. Thus the issue is not one of principle, but one of whether apartheid is sufficiently repugnant to deserve such action, and if so, how and how much.

In practice, the first rounds of sanctions need cost very little. Indeed, southern African government ministers have stressed that Britain and the US should start out by choosing those sanctions which cost them least and South Africa most. Bans on imports of fruit, krugerrands, and other South African goods cost Britain nothing. Nor do service bans, such as on airline landing rights, and sports and cultural boycotts. Bans on *new* investment and new loans also cost nothing. Enforcing the oil and arms embargoes would also not cost Britain and the US very much. That package alone would go a long way to put pressure on the Pretoria government.

Undoubtedly, sanctions beyond these first rounds would hurt the US and Britain, as well as South Africa. But at that stage other considerations come into play. If the Pretoria government continued to hold out, then the risk of a bitter and violent revolution would be much higher. In such a conflagration, Britain and the US could find much of their investment destroyed or at least nationalized. Rather than run the risk of losing everything, perhaps it would be better to make an 'investment' – to forgo profits and even jobs now to bring about the political change that might prevent a much greater loss later. But this requires a fundamental change in

South African policy. And as Geldenhuys pointed out, such a change cannot be obtained by 'actions which the target state would consider to be mere irritants or annoyances'.

Chapter Sixteen

Paying the price

South Africa's war against its neighbours often seems diffuse and hidden, but it has extracted an awesome toll. More than 100,000 people have been killed in Mozambique, plus thousands in Angola and hundreds elsewhere. Probably more than one million people have been displaced in Angola, Zambia, and Mozambique.

For the most part, the majority-ruled states of the region have been too busy fighting the war to keep score, but SADCC estimated in a report to the OAU in mid-1985 that in the first five years of its existence (1980–84 inclusive) destabilization has cost its members £7,000 million. Direct war damage accounts for £1,100 million of that. Higher transport costs plus the direct costs of South Africa's sanctions against its neighbours add £850 million. Production and exports lost due to destabilization are also about £850 million. Caring for one million refugees has cost more than £400 million. Higher military budgets caused by the need to defend against South Africa add £2,000 million. Most of the rest is accounted for by economic growth that has been lost because money that would have been invested in industry and other infrastructure has instead been spent on war.

The most frightening aspect of all is that the cost is rising rapidly – in 1984 alone it was roughly £2,500 million. Thus it is fair to assume that from the founding of SADCC in early 1980 to the publication of this book in early 1986, destabilization will have cost the majority-ruled states nearly £10,000 million. To put this figure into context: this is more than all the foreign aid given to SADCC states during those six years. And as SADCC noted in its report to the OAU, it 'only costed bricks and mortar, steel and machinery. There is no price for blood, no cost that can be assigned to the thousands who have died as a result of actions instigated and supported by apartheid.'

Cost of sanctions

The majority-ruled states will also pay a price for sanctions, boycotts, and disinvestment. But as SADCC noted in its report, if sanctions 'accelerate the ending of apartheid it would be well worth the additional cost'. In practice, for the neighbouring states, *sanctions are an investment* in ending apartheid.

During 1985, much was made by South Africa and by the British foreign office, among others, about the cost of sanctions to the neighbours. Indeed, as I have tried to show, one of South Africa's goals is to ensure that this is true. In response to this, the frontline heads of state made their position clear at a meeting in Maputo on 15 September 1985, when they unequivocally and unanimously backed international pressure for sanctions. The other three states who are members of SADCC but not the frontline states have taken various positions. King Moshoeshoe II of Lesotho travelled to the SADCC summit in Arusha on 9 August 1985 to make a moving plea: 'The effects of sanctions will call for great sacrifices among our peoples. We cannot stand against the sanctions campaign; thus we call upon the rest of the world that as it exercises what it feels to be a moral obligation, it should . . . increase support to SADCC states so as to cushion the indirect effects of sanctions to us.' Malawi has been silent, and pointedly not opposed sanctions, despite pressure from South Africa. Only Swaziland has opposed sanctions. Thus the position is clear and unambiguous. The 'Overview' paper for the January 1986 SADCC conference in Harare stresses that 'SADCC has repeatedly called on the international community to use its influence to deter and halt South African aggression and economic destabilization against its neighbours.' It goes on to note that 'several states individually or collectively have instituted economic sanctions against South Africa. SADCC member states encourage these initiatives, and urge that more effective measures be implemented.' The majority-ruled states of the region do not want the impact of sanctions on them to be used as an excuse not to impose sanctions. Indeed, as SADCC said in its paper to the OAU, 'those who are concerned about the negative effects of sanctions on the neighbouring states should provide assistance to these states to minimize the impact'.

Most sanctions would, in fact, have little *direct* effect on the SADCC states, and could benefit them. Disinvestment cannot hurt and would be directly beneficial if some of that money was invested in the neighbouring states instead. The arms and technology embargoes can only help by reducing the power of the apartheid military machine. A tighter oil embargo should not hurt, because the SADCC states could buy on the world market, in particular from Angola. Sports, cultural, and airline boycotts have no effect on the neighbouring states.

Two sanctions could have ripple effects. If the west really did stop buying South African minerals, it would reduce the need for migrant miners. And if the west stopped selling essential raw materials to South Africa, this would also stop it from selling to the neighbours goods made from those raw materials; again, however, the SADCC states could buy those goods on the world market, and often at a lower price, so it would help them to reorient their trade.

The real price of sanctions will come from South African retaliation. Two sorts have already been threatened by South Africa – expulsion of migrant miners and cutting off transport links. The former would be disastrous for Lesotho, but would not have an impossible impact on the other states. Cutting transport could isolate several states and cause some problems – but those states are only using South African ports and railways because South African commandos, the MNR, and Unita have sabotaged railways in Mozambique and Angola. Without that sabotage, the neighbouring states would not need or want to use South Africa.

Two other forms of retaliation also seem likely. As South Africa has already shown, it is prepared to close the borders with Lesotho. If it also expelled the miners, it would effectively make Lesotho a hostage. All three members of the customs union (Botswana, Lesotho, and Swaziland) would be subject to substantial economic pressure; South Africa would surely use the customs union to try to prevent them imposing sanctions. Also, as most of their trade is with South Africa, they would be most hit by embargoes on raw materials and spares for South Africa.

Finally, South Africa has shown its willingness to retaliate militarily. This would probably take four forms:

● To make its retaliation against transport links effective, South African troops would surely step up the pressure on rail links, especially those close to South Africa such as the lines from Maputo to Swaziland and Zimbabwe.

● Similarly, South Africa has shown its desire to control fuel supplies. Commandos would surely attack tank farms and pipelines throughout the region; it would do its best to prevent the three customs union members from buying oil elsewhere, and try to cut supplies to those states which already do not buy from South Africa.

● Inevitably, support for the surrogate armies would be increased, causing further economic and social disruption.

● South Africa would try to ensure its own critical supplies. During its five-year occupations its troops ran the Ruacana hydroelectricity project in Angola, after the Angolans declined to supply power from it to Namibia. If there were reasonably tight sanctions, South African troops would probably take over Ruacana again, the Highland Water Scheme in Lesotho (when it is built), and the railway through Swaziland. They might also take over the Cahora Bassa Dam in Mozambique. And if Anglo American's interests in the Botswana diamond mines (the largest in the region) were threatened, South Africa might occupy them as well.

Help is essential

Thus international action to support the majority-ruled states must be two-fold: sanctions *plus* help for the neighbouring states to assist them to resist South African retaliation.

Lesotho is a special case. Clearly any international boycotts and sanctions would exclude Lesotho, but Pretoria is likely to take it hostage. Julius Nyerere, the recently retired president of Tanzania, warned that a Berlin-style airlift may be needed for Lesotho.

Compensation for lost migrant wages will be needed. This could take the form of development projects to provide alternative jobs. Compensation for lost customs union payments may also be required.

South Africa itself has targeted transport as a key area. Substantial foreign aid will be needed to repair damage already done to the railways, and to upgrade and rehabilitate them to carry the cargo which now passes through South Africa.

Trade arrangements will be disrupted, and some help will be needed, perhaps in the form of a revolving credit fund to encourage SADCC states to trade with each other. Another form of assistance would be credit for SADCC states to buy Angolan oil. In practice, any assistance to SADCC will strengthen the neighbouring states' ability to resist South African destabilization.

Finally, the fraught issue of military help must be faced. So far the west has been extremely reluctant to provide military help to the majority-ruled states. Yet South Africa will surely attack oil supplies, transport links, and other key points. If the neighbouring states' capacities to defend themselves are not strengthened, then South African retaliation will extract an unacceptable price. Military assistance must be a central part of any sanctions and compensation package.

Ending the war

There is a war going on in southern Africa – a war for the control of the majority-ruled states. Despite its high cost, it has remained a largely hidden war, overshadowed by events inside South Africa. But white South Africa has decided to defend apartheid by fighting the war outside first, and the cost in death and destruction is so far much higher outside than inside the country. Pretoria's war against its neighbours will end only with the destruction of apartheid.

White South Africa sees the war outside as a second front in the internal battle to defend apartheid against majority rule. Thus the neighbouring states *are* the frontline of the war against apartheid. If apartheid is to be destroyed, that frontline must be held and strengthened.

Further reading

A longer and much more detailed discussion of the material in this book, with full references, is contained in:
Hanlon, Joseph, *Beggar Your Neighbours*, CIIR and James Currey (to be published in 1986).

Many, although not all, of the events mentioned in this book were reported in the press at the time. There is a fortnightly newsletter which contains most of the relevant press clippings on southern Africa, and which provides a particularly useful way to keep up with events in the region. It costs £25 or $40 per year. It is published in the Netherlands, but is almost completely in English:
Facts and Reports (OZ Achterburgwal 173, 1012 DJ Amsterdam, The Netherlands).

There are also a variety of yearbooks which look at the individual countries of Africa. Some also regularly feature articles on southern Africa, including:
Legum, Colin (ed.), *Africa Contemporary Record*, Africana (Holmes & Meier), London.

In addition, there are fortnightly newsletters of reports from the Mozambican and Angolan government press agencies:
Mozambique Information Office News Review (7a Caledonian Rd, London N1 9DX – £10 in UK, £18 outside).
Angop News Bulletin (16 Maddox Street, London W1).

For further reading on the two countries most severely hit by destabilization:

Wolfers, Michael, and Bergerol, Jane, *Angola in the Front Line*, Zed, 1983.

Hanlon, Joseph, *Mozambique: The Revolution under Fire*, Zed, 1984.

Finally, for more on South Africa and the struggle against apartheid:

Omond, Roger, *The Apartheid Handbook*, Penguin, 1985.

Davies, Rob, and others, *The Struggle for South Africa*, Zed, 1984.

South Africa in the 1980s, Catholic Institute for International Relations, 1986.

South African Review, Ravan, Johannesburg, published annually.

Index

MORE ABOUT PENGUINS, PELICANS, PEREGRINES AND PUFFINS

For further information about books available from Penguins please write to Dept EP, Penguin Books Ltd, Harmondsworth, Middlesex UB7 0DA.

In the U.S.A.: For a complete list of books available from Penguins in the United States write to Dept DG, Penguin Books, 299 Murray Hill Parkway, East Rutherford, New Jersey 07073.

In Canada: For a complete list of books available from Penguins in Canada write to Penguin Books Canada Ltd, 2801 John Street, Markham, Ontario L3R 1B4.

In Australia: For a complete list of books available from Penguins in Australia write to the Marketing Department, Penguin Books Australia Ltd, P.O. Box 257, Ringwood, Victoria 3134.

In New Zealand: For a complete list of books available from Penguins in New Zealand write to the Marketing Department, Penguin Books (N.Z.) Ltd, Private Bag, Takapuna, Auckland 9.

In India: For a complete list of books available from Penguins in India write to Penguin Overseas Ltd, 706 Eros Apartments, 56 Nehru Place, New Delhi 11019.

A CHOICE OF
PELICANS AND PEREGRINES

☐ *The Knight, the Lady and the Priest*
Georges Duby   £6.95

The acclaimed study of the making of modern marriage in medieval France. 'He has traced this story – sometimes amusing, often horrifying, always startling – in a series of brilliant vignettes' – *Observer*

☐ *The Limits of Soviet Power* **Jonathan Steele**   £3.95

The Kremlin's foreign policy – Brezhnev to Chernenko, is discussed in this informed, informative 'wholly invaluable and extraordinarily timely study' – *Guardian*

☐ *Understanding Organizations* **Charles B. Handy**   £4.95

Third Edition. Designed as a practical source-book for managers, this Pelican looks at the concepts, key issues and current fashions in tackling organizational problems.

☐ *The Pelican Freud Library: Volume 12*   £5.95

Containing the major essays: *Civilization, Society and Religion, Group Psychology* and *Civilization and Its Discontents*, plus other works.

☐ *Windows on the Mind* **Erich Harth**   £4.95

Is there a physical explanation for the various phenomena that we call 'mind'? Professor Harth takes in age-old philosophers as well as the latest neuroscientific theories in his masterly study of memory, perception, free will, selfhood, sensation and other richly controversial fields.

☐ *The Pelican History of the World*
J. M. Roberts   £5.95

'A stupendous achievement . . . This is the unrivalled World History for our day' – A. J. P. Taylor

A CHOICE OF
PELICANS AND PEREGRINES

☐ *A Question of Economics* **Peter Donaldson** £4.95

Twenty key issues – from the City and big business to trades unions – clarified and discussed by Peter Donaldson, author of *10 × Economics* and one of our greatest popularizers of economics.

☐ *Inside the Inner City* **Paul Harrison** £4.95

A report on urban poverty and conflict by the author of *Inside the Third World*. 'A major piece of evidence' – *Sunday Times*. 'A classic: it tells us what it is really like to be poor, and why' – *Time Out*

☐ *What Philosophy Is* **Anthony O'Hear** £4.95

What are human beings? How should people act? How do our thoughts and words relate to reality? Contemporary attitudes to these age-old questions are discussed in this new study, an eloquent and brilliant introduction to philosophy today.

☐ *The Arabs* **Peter Mansfield** £4.95

New Edition. 'Should be studied by anyone who wants to know about the Arab world and how the Arabs have become what they are today' – *Sunday Times*

☐ *Religion and the Rise of Capitalism*
R. H. Tawney £3.95

The classic study of religious thought of social and economic issues from the later middle ages to the early eighteenth century.

☐ *The Mathematical Experience*
Philip J. Davis and Reuben Hersh £7.95

Not since *Gödel, Escher, Bach* has such an entertaining book been written on the relationship of mathematics to the arts and sciences. 'It deserves to be read by everyone ... an instant classic' – *New Scientist*

A CHOICE OF PENGUINS

☐ *The Complete Penguin Stereo Record and Cassette Guide*
Greenfield, Layton and March   £7.95

A new edition, now including information on compact discs. 'One of the few indispensables on the record collector's bookshelf' – *Gramophone*

☐ *Selected Letters of Malcolm Lowry*
Edited by Harvey Breit and Margerie Bonner Lowry £5.95

'Lowry emerges from these letters not only as an extremely interesting man, but also a lovable one' – Philip Toynbee

☐ *The First Day on the Somme*
Martin Middlebrook   £3.95

1 July 1916 was the blackest day of slaughter in the history of the British Army. 'The soldiers receive the best service a historian can provide: their story told in their own words' – *Guardian*

☐ *A Better Class of Person* **John Osborne**   £2.50

The playwright's autobiography, 1929–56. 'Splendidly enjoyable' – John Mortimer. 'One of the best, richest and most bitterly truthful autobiographies that I have ever read' – Melvyn Bragg

☐ *The Winning Streak* **Goldsmith and Clutterbuck**   £2.95

Marks & Spencer, Saatchi & Saatchi, United Biscuits, GEC . . . The UK's top companies reveal their formulas for success, in an important and stimulating book that no British manager can afford to ignore.

☐ *The First World War* **A. J. P. Taylor**   £4.95

'He manages in some 200 illustrated pages to say almost everything that is important . . . A special text . . . a remarkable collection of photographs' – *Observer*

A CHOICE OF PENGUINS

☐ *Man and the Natural World* **Keith Thomas**   £4.95

Changing attitudes in England, 1500–1800. 'An encyclopedic study of man's relationship to animals and plants . . . a book to read again and again' – Paul Theroux, *Sunday Times* Books of the Year

☐ *Jean Rhys: Letters 1931–66*
  Edited by Francis Wyndham and Diana Melly   £4.95

'Eloquent and invaluable . . . her life emerges, and with it a portrait of an unexpectedly indomitable figure' – Marina Warner in the *Sunday Times*

☐ *The French Revolution* **Christopher Hibbert**   £4.95

'One of the best accounts of the Revolution that I know . . . Mr Hibbert is outstanding' – J. H. Plumb in the *Sunday Telegraph*

☐ *Isak Dinesen* **Judith Thurman**   £4.95

The acclaimed life of Karen Blixen, 'beautiful bride, disappointed wife, radiant lover, bereft and widowed woman, writer, sibyl, Scheherazade, child of Lucifer, Baroness; always a unique human being . . . an assiduously researched and finely narrated biography' – *Books & Bookmen*

☐ *The Amateur Naturalist*
  Gerald Durrell with Lee Durrell   £4.95

'Delight . . . on every page . . . packed with authoritative writing, learning without pomposity . . . it represents a real bargain' – *The Times Educational Supplement*. 'What treats are in store for the average British household' – *Daily Express*

☐ *When the Wind Blows* **Raymond Briggs**   £2.95

'A visual parable against nuclear war: all the more chilling for being in the form of a strip cartoon' – *Sunday Times*. 'The most eloquent anti-Bomb statement you are likely to read' – *Daily Mail*

PENGUIN REFERENCE BOOKS

☐ **The Penguin Dictionary of Troublesome Words**   £2.50

A witty, straightforward guide to the pitfalls and hotly disputed issues in standard written English, illustrated with examples and including a glossary of grammatical terms and an appendix on punctuation.

☐ **The Penguin Guide to the Law**   £8.95

This acclaimed reference book is designed for everyday use, and forms the most comprehensive handbook ever published on the law as it affects the individual.

☐ **The Penguin Dictionary of Religions**   £4.95

The rites, beliefs, gods and holy books of all the major religions throughout the world are covered in this book, which is illustrated with charts, maps and line drawings.

☐ **The Penguin Medical Encyclopedia**   £4.95

Covers the body and mind in sickness and in health, including drugs, surgery, history, institutions, medical vocabulary and many other aspects. Second Edition. 'Highly commendable' – *Journal of the Institute of Health Education*

☐ **The Penguin Dictionary of Physical Geography**   £4.95

This book discusses all the main terms used, in over 5,000 entries illustrated with diagrams and meticulously cross-referenced.

☐ **Roget's Thesaurus**   £3.50

Specially adapted for Penguins, Sue Lloyd's acclaimed new version of Roget's original will help you find the right words for your purposes. 'As normal a part of an intelligent household's library as the Bible, Shakespeare or a dictionary' – *Daily Telegraph*